Religion That Is Eternal

Other Books by
G. Ray Jordan

PRAYER THAT PREVAILS   ADVENTURES IN RADIANT LIVING

BEYOND DESPAIR   WE FACE CALVARY—AND LIFE!

YOU CAN PREACH!   FAITH THAT PROPELS

THE EMERGING REVIVAL   COURAGE THAT PROPELS

THE SUPREME POSSESSION   INTIMATE INTERESTS OF YOUTH

WE BELIEVE   THE INTOLERANCE OF CHRISTIANITY

LOOK AT THE STARS!   WHAT IS YOURS?

WHY THE CROSS?   THE HOUR HAS COME

Religion That Is Eternal

by G. Ray Jordan

NEW YORK THE MACMILLAN COMPANY 1960

First Printing

The Macmillan Company, New York
Brett-Macmillan Ltd., Galt, Ontario

Printed in the United States of America

Library of Congress catalog card number: 60–8121

To CAROLINE with Love

Preface

In this book it is my purpose to face those changes in our world which are so momentous that it is difficult at present to evaluate them properly or to grasp their significance. At the same time, most of us can see how seriously they are affecting our lives. Religion cannot escape—is not now evading—the many problems posed by this age of space explorations, intercontinental missiles, and hydrogen bombs.

Many who are not able to frame their feelings in adequate language nevertheless sense the fact that religion, specifically Christianity, must face these issues. The urgency of our day demands daring adventures in the area of the spiritual. Indeed, there are those who anticipate that the greatest discoveries of our century will be in this very field.

It is my desire to emphasize those principles for life which are eternal. Furthermore, I am eager to reaffirm the assurance of Christ that dependable help is available. We are offered resources which have been adequate for hosts of people, who can testify to their validity and dependability.

The stepped-up speed of transportation, communication, and present-day scientific developments do not deny the basic need for what religion at its highest can do for us. Quite to the contrary, these contemporary conditions underscore demands for that which only great ethical religion can do—most of all, what *God* can do.

When disappointment, disillusionment, and defeat come, we look for resources with which to meet them. When what we have does not satisfy us, it is logical to seek something better. Fortunately, we can experience a response to our deepest longings, for God is our Friend.

This truth can be demonstrated. It is my purpose, therefore, in the pages that follow, to show *how* we can experience religion that we will never outgrow, and thus *how* we can accept the gifts of God, receive His benefits, and learn the practical meaning of His presence and power.

G. R. J.

Contents

I. Religion We Will Never Outgrow   1

II. What Is Really Important   13

III. What We Need Most   26

IV. Wise Men Worship   40

V. We Claim What Is Ours   55

VI. We Know Where We Are Going   68

VII. If Our Homes Survive   79

VIII. We Take Christ Seriously   96

IX. A Faith That Sings   109

X. God Can Really Meet Our Needs!   121

I

Religion We Will Never Outgrow

Many people think we are ready to discard religion. Some feel we have outgrown it, just as we outgrow an old suit of clothes, and then dispose of it, since it is no longer in style, or usable.

One of the explanations for this attitude is the speeded-up tempo of life. The dizzy pace at which we have been moving in the past few years has brought so many changes that hosts of people feel religion itself has been seriously affected. Large numbers, to be sure, hold a suspended sentence with respect to the worth of religion, but are nevertheless troubled by world conditions. And, of course, many more act on the idea that religion is outdated than express their thoughts with open frankness.

1. Changes We Face

Certainly our world is in a state of change—one so great that few of us can grasp what is happening. This fact would be trite were it not almost terrifying. The facetious references we make to it merely serve to emphasize our scientific progress. Even those

1

who face life in a superficial manner are at least partially
aware of these stupendous developments. We cannot ignore
them.

Whether we view world conditions superficially or seriously,
the facts are such that we cannot escape all consideration of their
significance. The fictional stories of Jules Verne, the French
author, are no longer figments of the imagination. It was in 1863
that he wrote *Five Weeks in a Balloon*. In 1872 *Around the
World in Eighty Days* was published. Our grandfathers used to
sprawl in front of open fireplaces and laugh hilariously at the
stories which sprang from the imaginative mind of this talented
writer. But Wiley Post "turned the trick" and won international
fame by flying around the world in seven days—and now his
record is so outdated we seldom refer to it.

Indeed, speed of travel has been stepped up to such a degree
that few of us can grasp what this actually means. Sometime ago
this was impressed on my mind, when we caught a plane after
midnight at Lod Airport, which serves Tel Aviv. We had breakfast in Rome, lunch in Paris, and dinner in London, and there
was still time that evening to enjoy one of Shakespeare's plays,
after I had completed plans for returning to the Continent. Since
then some of our jet fliers have circled the globe in a day. Space
travel is no longer the fictional phase of science.

Then there is communication. See what has happened to it!
When Henry M. Stanley found David Livingstone, he was at a
little village called Ujiji, on the shore of Lake Tanganyika. Mr.
Stanley handed the missionary a batch of mail, in which there
were some letters postmarked two years earlier in London. Now
there is a radio station at Ujiji, and engineers tell us that it is
possible for a word to be sent from London to Ujiji in two-fifths
of a second. Although most of us do not understand the technical
principles involved, we readily accept their statement.

These are but symbols and suggestions of numerous scientific
advances which lead many people to feel that religion will never

be the same again. They apparently compel others to assume
that there is not too much abiding value in the entire content of
religion, since certain emphases of the Mid-Victorian church are
outmoded. Others jump to the conclusion that worship itself is outdated.

Instead of either hastily denying this assertion or becoming
so emotionally upset about it that we enter angrily into an argu-
mentative mood, let us consider some values that obviously will
not be lost, regardless of what happens *to* our world—or *in* our
world. These are tremendously important, and they are related
vitally to the deepest meaning of Christianity.

II. Christian Courtesy

Beginning with the simple matter of thoughtfulness for others,
which involves courtesy, it becomes increasingly clear that here
is something that we can never abandon, without sustaining losses
of an inestimable character. Gracious regard for other people is
one of the real needs of life. It always has been. Samuel Johnson
once put it this way: "A man has no more right to say a rude thing
to another than to knock him down." When we remember certain
statements which Mr. Johnson made to some individuals in moments of impatience, this affirmation becomes even more significant!

An incident in John Wesley's life underscores the practical
importance of this attitude. One day after he had preached on
a village green, Mr. Wesley was invited to take lunch at the home
of a wealthy Methodist. (There were not too many such people
then!) Several other guests, including preachers and residents
of the village, were present. A local preacher was seated next
to the daughter of the host. The young lady was noted for her
extraordinary beauty and charm. She also liked luxury. On her
hand were several rings—perhaps too many. The thoughtless
visitor, who was seated next to her, seized the hand of the young
lady in a very abrupt manner. Catching Mr. Wesley's eye, he

loudly inquired, "What do you think of this, sir, for a Methodist hand?" The girl turned crimson. Everyone knew Mr. Wesley's aversion to finery. It has been written of him that when he died, he left a silver spoon, a much-abused reputation, a well-worn pulpit gown, and the Methodist Church. On this occasion, however, the aged evangelist showed a tact which Chesterfield himself might have coveted. Looking up kindly, he smilingly said, "The hand is very beautiful."

Regard for others has now taken on an even more meaningful significance. "The courtesy of the highway" and "the courtesy of the airlanes" are expressions familiar to us because they are used daily. They emphasize how indispensable consideration of other people is today. When thoughtful regard for our fellow human beings would prevent some thirty-five thousand deaths on the highways each year, we can see that this characteristic is needed as never before.

In the airlanes pilots who are without concern for other aircraft constitute a menace. This can result in terrifying disasters. Some time ago, when we were flying from Europe to New York, this was etched upon our minds. After dinner in Shannon, Ireland, as we were settling down for the transatlantic passage, the captain of our plane asked for attention. He stated that, as we knew, we were scheduled to fly to Gander. He informed us that the weather over this area was not good. For this reason, in order to give the passengers a comfortable flight, it had been decided to fly by way of Iceland to New York. Thus we would avoid the storm over the Atlantic.

Some hours later, when we landed at Iceland to refuel, as we walked to the terminal we passed plane after plane. Most of the great airlines were represented. They had also changed their course, and for the same reason: the comfort and safety of the passengers.

Suppose some of those pilots had not courteously obeyed

directions of the officials in charge of all transatlantic flights. Suppose some had decided to fly as they pleased. Hundreds of lives could have been lost. Numbers of planes would never have arrived at their destinations.

Of course, courtesy is not only gentleness. It is that—and more! It is kindness which makes us recognize our spiritual relationship to others. At its highest, and in its finest expression, it shows our kinship to God.

For, as A. E. Whitham has reminded us, God constantly portrays divine courtesy. Jesus referred to this when he said: "He maketh his sun to rise on the evil and on the good, and sendeth rain on the just and on the unjust" (Matthew 5:45). This is, indeed, the courtesy of God.

Christ's own tenderness springs from the truest kindness. For this reason it is so very tough! It does not change its nature easily—it can stand terrific pressure. Those who feel that Christianity is not capable of handling our contemporary world do not understand its spiritual fiber. The tenderness of God is enduring. Therefore it is not changed by the rudeness or discourtesy or evil of people. Jesus portrayed this gracious spirit unfailingly. That is why it is possible to interpret Christlikeness in an adequate way only when we think of Christian courtesy.

III. Christian Comradeship

Understanding this quality of Christianity, we readily recognize the abiding value of divine comradeship. "Henceforth I call you . . . friends" (John 15:15). Jesus' words come to have deep significance. The friendship he offers is everlasting. No matter how far we travel, or whatever occurs during our treks to distant places, friendship is a requisite for any genuine sense of satisfaction.

There is no fellowship of the finest sort which is not always characterized by integrity and dependability. Only so does it have lasting quality. Robert Burns lamented that he could not pour out his soul to another without some sad day regretting it. His reason? He was fearful that he would be betrayed. This is the antithesis of the comradeship which Jesus offers.

Socrates, too, was keenly aware of his need of friends who were loyal and true. His reason for constructing a small home in Athens is explained by this fact. An acquaintance asked why he was building such a little residence. His immediate reply was that if he could fill the house with true friends, he would consider himself adequately accommodated.

We escape loneliness when, through Christian prayer, we find a friend capable of sharing with us strength and dependability. These simple lines express the deep desires of so many people:

> Lord, when the evening closes,
> And I stand with eager fearful hands
> Toward Heaven's far shore,
> Bring me no gift of roses,
> As the sands run out
> To run again for me no more.
> But give me one clear hour at close of day,
> And whisper as the darkling shadows fall,
> The names of friends I lost along the way,
> The faithful friends I can no more recall.
> Then, while on my lips their names are set,
> Oh, speed the silent tides that I must stem,
> That ere again I slumber or forget,
> I may begin my eager quest of them.

No matter what happens to us, or to our world, each of us always wants to escape the pain of loneliness and the inevitable feeling of emptiness which results when we are without those who care. For friendship, when it is true, makes it possible for heart to meet heart, without delay and inconvenience of preliminaries.

Prayer is our means of cultivating that friendship with God. With it all life gains meaning, and we are at home.

IV. Confidence in God

So, when we truly begin to understand faith, we know that it is no fad! It is something that we shall never outgrow. There are conditions, to be sure, in our world which force us to face many undesirable facts. There are those who talk glibly about religion being seriously influenced by these. But confidence, which is the result of comradeship with God, is an experience for which all of us long, when we are at our best. Augustine stated it more graphically than most of us could, but not more dramatically than the facts justify. For, we *are* restless until we rest in God. No matter what conditions or circumstances we face, belief in the Being who created us, as well as the world in which we live, is a constant requisite for life.

So, faith at its highest and finest is trust in a divine Friend. Indeed, it is not *what,* but *whom* we believe. This is what John Oxenham came to see so clearly, "for Christ is more than all the creeds" of men. He is our one never-failing friend.

We must have the assurance Christ brings when he tells us of God. For it does not matter whether a loved one is thrown from a car or whether we face the tragedy of the loss of a comrade resulting from the crash of a plane, each of us needs confidence in a God we can trust. Whether our little child, whom we dearly love, falls into a well at the farm and loses his life, or is run over by a speeding hot-rod driver, in either event we need the knowledge that the universe is not an irresponsible machine. We desperately want the assurance that there is a Being in whom we can place our trust, One who eventually can bind up our broken hearts, and make it possible for us to face a new day of hope and light and love. A God who is both worthy of adoration and capable of helping us is a requisite for life—regardless of what happens to us. Indeed, when the social, political, and economic orders change, it becomes even more imperative for us to be sure that the great spiritual experiences remain—that they are valid and always relevant.

Digging in the ruins of ancient Egypt, some archaeologists had this truth forced upon their minds when they uncovered the sarcophagus of a little child. When they were able to interpret the words written on the luxurious casket, they were moved by the pain of the father who centuries before had written, "Oh, my life, my love, my little one—would God I had died for thee!" Three thousand years ago a father was pained too keenly to express adequately the loss he had sustained. Three thousand years from now, if we have not destroyed our world with intercontinental ballistic missiles, and if there are still those who stop to think and care and love, our children's children will be pained by the losses they sustain. The poignant pain of the broken heart is not eased by any mechanical device.

V. Constancy of Christian Character

Just as we must be sure of the guidance of a God who is able to take care of our truest needs, regardless of the kind of world in which we live, so does our dependability which springs from devotion to the Divine become essential. Our own integrity is evidence of our belief in God's character. It also portrays a relationship we can never afford to lose.

The well-known characters in Daniel caught something of the greatness of this attitude when they declared: ". . . our God whom we serve is able to deliver us . . . , and he will deliver us out of thine hand, O king. But if not, be it known unto thee, O king, that we will not serve thy gods, nor worship the golden image which thou hast set up" (Daniel 3:17–18).

With this kind of devotion we discover that the faith which we keep keeps us. "Thanks be to God, which giveth us the victory through our Lord Jesus Christ" (I Corinthians 15:57). This is not dogma, as we know it. As has well been pointed out, dogma may now be the dead faith of the living, but once it was the living faith of the dead. Here, therefore, is something that is actually alive, and will always be vital.

Arnold J. Toynbee describes a relevant incident which took place about fourteen hundred years ago in the capital city of a great empire. There were turmoil, civil war, and fighting in the streets of the city. Toynbee writes: "The emperor of that empire was holding council to decide whether he should carry on the struggle or whether he should take ship and sail away to safety." At the crown council, his wife, the empress, was present. The famous historian records graphically the decision of this woman: "You, Justinian, can sail away if you like; the ship is at the quay and the sea is open; but I am going to stay and see it out. . . ." [1]

Some of us would like to speak—and live—in that same spirit. For no matter what happens to our contemporary social order, or what affects Western civilization, here we recognize devotion with the touch of divinity. On its highest level, it is an indication of the Christian interpretation of integrity. Indeed, it presents a conception of religious loyalty that we shall never outgrow.

This makes possible the "unpurchasable man"—which is manifestly a present desperate need of our nation, of society, of the church, and of the world. Certainly to the degree that we cultivate faithfulness and dependability ourselves, we can have the assurance of a Deity in whom we confidently place our trust.

Stevenson has depicted this in his story of an old sea rover. A youth was fleeing from a tragedy which seemed about to doom his city. As he ran toward an older man, the fugitive shouted that the temple was burning and that Thor—their god—was being slain. "Hurry! Hurry!" cried the frightened young man, "if you would escape." The old rover, who was headed toward the city, hesitated a moment. Then, quickly sizing up the situation, he took his

[1] *Civilization on Trial* (New York, Oxford University Press, 1948), p. 225. Used by permission.

battle-ax off his shoulder and rubbed his thumb along the edge of it. Then he was off. "Where are you going?" cried the astonished youth. As the old rover hastened on toward the city, he shouted back: "I? Oh, I am going back to die with God!" If we lose this spirit, we do not outgrow anything; we shrivel up!

Something like this loyalty is ours when we are sure that the Being who runs the universe is in character like the person who died on Calvary's cross. In our best moments we too shout to those about us who look questioningly in our faces: "Where am I going? Oh, I am going back to be with Christ on Calvary!" Even when we do not feel that we dare die as did he, in our finest hours we know that the devotion which we express in our presence with him on Golgotha is itself something that the world will never outgrow, something we can never outlive.

VI. Concern for Mankind

If we find this kind of assurance, and to this degree accept reality in religion, we shall discover that we share at least something of the same concern for all of our comrades which characterizes Christ himself.

When we fulfill the purpose of faith, faith becomes a force which fulfills the purpose of our lives. This explains why the distance of our *outreach* and the length of our *downreach* measure, with precision, the height of our *upreach*. Those who have the most sensitive feeling for their fellows, which is the result of their faith in life, because of their confidence in God, discover that this can come to fulfillment in attitude and spirit toward mankind. Here is something we shall never outgrow, for ultimate reality is seen in Christ, and attitudes which were his can become ours.

We may not use the language of George Williams, the founder of the Y.M.C.A., but we can understand his motive and spirit. When he was past eighty, and his mind had begun to wander a bit, he was still engrossed by the cause that had captured him. John R. Mott tells us that Mr. Williams asked him, "Are you ever thrown into contact with a man without speaking to him about Jesus Christ?" Whether we use the technique of George Williams, or some other devotee of Christ, our lives will always witness to the same concern.

So we can appreciate what General Booth had in mind when, vividly presenting the story of his past experiences, in St. Louis a number of years ago, he reached a dramatic conclusion by exclaiming: "That is what I did with my life. . . . What are you doing with yours?"

SUMMARY

I. Some attitudes are of abiding value.

We never outgrow them—and time never diminishes their
value.

II. *Courtesy* is a requirement if we are to live safely or satisfactorily.

It was never needed more than it is today.

III. *Friends* who *understand* make life worth living—any time,
anywhere.

Problems are most difficult to handle without them.

IV. *Faith* in a Supreme Friend, God, brings inner strength.

No matter what else one has, this is essential!

V. *Faithfulness* to our highest sense of right

Gives security and poise.

We keep faith only as we live faithfully.

VI. *Happiness* is the by-product of fulfilling our faith.

This joy we can keep, regardless of conditions around us.

II

What Is Really Important

"Life can be a masterpiece, a mixture, or a mess." This assertion of Joseph Fort Newton is confirmed by all human experience. Furthermore, we are deciding daily exactly which it will be for us. The hour of decision is *now*. By choosing what is first in our lives, we determine what life brings us. Inevitably, therefore, whenever we fail to discriminate between mere things and those higher values that abide, we miss life itself.

I. Physical Safety

Even in our daily physical relationships, we must answer the question, "What must I do to be sure of life?" Here is an inescapable issue, since each of us does decide what he thinks is really important. This holds true in the area of physical safety. It is, indeed, a daily decision.

This was etched on my mind a few years ago, when some of us were making an automobile trip through the state of New York. We came to a little town in the western part of the state.

Late in the afternoon, as we drove into a village, there was so much excitement that we found ourselves nervously asking what was going on. Quickly we learned that there had been an automobile wreck. One man was killed, and others had been severely hurt.

A passenger in the car explained how the accident occurred. A bee had flown into the automobile as the group was riding toward the village. Fearing the bee might sting him, the driver attempted to brush him out of the car. As he made an effort with his hand to do so, he lost control of the wheel. There was a swerve, a crash—and the driver was dead. Others in the car were injured.

Reconstructing the incident, we can easily understand how it occurred, for normally a bee is certainly an undesirable "hitchhiker"! When the insect stings, he can cause extreme discomfort. Nevertheless, it is obviously preferable to be pained by the sting of a bee than it is to lose your life. The incident is a vivid example of the kind of occurrence that requires quick decisions which we must make almost spontaneously.

A fire which destroyed a theater in one of our cities happened while a traveling road company was presenting its performance. Turmoil followed the shout of "Fire"! In the excitement one of the chorus girls, who had temporarily escaped to safety, rushed back into the burning building to save her clothes. She was trapped by the flames and suffocated by the smoke. Escape was impossible; she perished in the fire.

All of us feel sorry for this young girl. Her life was doubtlessly difficult—at best a paltry one. Very likely, practically all she owned after years of struggle was a cheap suitcase, filled with clothes. But she is not the first individual who lost her life by risking it for a mere trifle.

We often make the same mistake by overemphasizing speed in travel. Most of us, to be sure, feel that rapid transportation is vital for present-day living. If, however, speed merely hastens us to the cemetery, it does not justify the high evaluation which so many of our contemporaries place on it. This much is clear.

Of course, we never acquire wisdom until we learn what is worthy of us—and of life. Thus do we cultivate the ability properly to judge both possessions and experiences.

Again and again each of us must focus on the tremendous difference between goods *for* life and *life itself*. Unfortunately we do not grasp this quickly in everyday relationships, unless we cultivate keen insight into the meaning of ordinary experiences. A newspaper story, which told of a man in the Midwest on his way home one night when he was suddenly beset by thieves, etches this on our minds. The reporter who described the incident related how the thieves attacked the man and then killed him. Writing with biting satire, far more acrid than he probably realized, he closed his account with this brief comment: "The man had little cash on his person. Thus practically all he lost was his life."

II. Mental Satisfaction

If we are to keep from losing the higher life, we must learn that mental satisfaction is contingent upon our being able to discern what is really important. Each day, indeed, each hour is a time of inevitable crisis and unavoidable decision.

The days are far more important than we realize. What we bring to them determines what they bring us.

Muffled and dumb the hypocritic days like barefoot dervishes,
    And walking single in an endless file,
Bear diadems and faggots in their hands.
    To each they offer gifts after his will—
Bread, kingdoms, stars, the sky that holds them all.
    I in my pleached garden watched the pomp,
Forgot my morning wishes, hastily took
    A few herbs and apples, and the day
Turned and departed, silent. I too late
    Under her solemn fillet saw the scorn.[1]

[1] From *The Manhood of the Master*, by Harry Emerson Fosdick (New York, Association Press, 1913), p. 137.

When we fail to see "the things that are more excellent," we make a mess of life. We miss its deepest satisfactions. A devotee of baseball compelled us to face this truth in an unexpected way. The time was 1954, when the Yankees lost the pennant. It is difficult, to be sure, for some people to believe that this team ever lost the pennant! Nevertheless, it did. With reference to this particular year, the Associated Press carried a story concerning a man in Florida who was so devoted to the New York Yankees that he could not stand the facetious references of his friends to the downfall of the baseball club. He could not take the "ribbing" they gave him. The account, carried by hundreds of newspapers, indicated that some of the man's acquaintances teased him so mercilessly that finally, unable to handle the problem of his nerves, he took his own life.

Certainly, winning a baseball game may be important to one's emotional satisfaction at the moment. There are, moreover, quite a few of us who hate to see our teams lose. But, after all, the kind of mental satisfaction that abides is of far more value than an athletic victory.

Because Esau failed to understand how vital the same basic choice is, he made such a tragic mistake. When it was too late, he saw how foolishly he had acted. Any man who despises his birthright because he is more interested in food is hardly in a position to anticipate continuing mental satisfaction.

Dealing with this characteristic, so essential to a meaningful life, a man with keen insight often asked, "If you were to receive a million dollars tomorrow, what would you do with it?" This was his way of discovering what really comes first in a person's desires.

Certainly, we have to agree that there is something less than high thinking on the part of college students who are more concerned about "fallout" at a dance than they are about the radio-active fallout of the A and H bombs. This ought to be crystal clear. Unfortunately, hosts of young people need much more moral insight and spiritual understanding in order to grasp the tremendous importance of this truth.

"What is really important?" is not just a serious question. Actually, it concerns our whole future. Although there are many vital issues of which we may think, the ultimate matter of supreme significance is in the decision we make with regard to relative and absolute values. Life constantly poses this critical choice.

III. Social Security

For the same reason, inevitably we make up our minds with reference to the meaning of social security. Here is an area of thought, and of life, which demands discernment of the keenest character. If, indeed, we discover what is truly important, we shall learn the worth of social security—with or without a number!

All of us desire to feel confident, whether we confess it or not. We want it for the social order of which we are a part, as well as for ourselves. Of course, the essential quality of any feeling of safety must be that it is justified.

That is why we are never comfortable so long as we realize that those who determine so much of the character of our social order have their values confused. No wonder hosts of people in one of our states were greatly disturbed when the legislature of that commonwealth spent *days* discussing whether there would be an enactment of certain "blue laws" preventing Sunday fishing, and then hastily curbed freedom of speech.

In spite of all the entertaining stories we may enjoy relevant to forms of recreation and indulgence on Sunday, there are serious facts with which we may have to deal. Is it not true that if we reason clearly, we are pained by the thought of insecurity when we are being guided in our legal and social relationships by superficial thinking? This is inevitable when so-called statesmen are more concerned with the illegality of recreation than they are about the supreme importance of freedom of speech, racial fairness, and social justice.

Indeed, any sense of security, either for us personally or for our social order, must be based upon concern for people everywhere. The kindly understanding and consideration of others is of supreme significance. It is essential to any sense of real security. No wonder Jesus exclaimed, "Make to yourselves friends of the mammon of unrighteousness" (Luke 16:9). Actually, it is the only way that we shall begin to understand eternal life in contemporary existence.

So, too, if we ever gain an adequate sense of safety, it will be necessary to appreciate and properly evaluate the home. We can, to be sure, abandon this institution. If we do, however, we shall doubtlessly face the final dissolution of society.

Smiling at contemporary conditions relevant to the supposed importance of the home will not prevent this from happening. When a real-estate dealer called upon a man recently to sell him a new house, he caught a glimpse of this truth. The prospective buyer greeted him with this statement: "I was born in a hospital. I went to school in a college. I courted in an automobile. I was married in a church. I eat in a cafeteria. I go to the golf course in the morning, baseball games in the afternoons, and see plays at night. I expect to be buried from an undertaker's establishment. What I need is not a home but a garage."

Over against this, recall some words of Grace Noll Crowell, who was so indebted to her early home life that she felt impelled to express it with delicate and tender appreciation, describing a lovely picture in her mind, so dear that it was as "clear-cut as a cameo." She remembers coming down a shady street, happy and carefree, "on lightly dancing feet," eagerly anticipating seeing her mother.

That is not nostalgic. It is not mere sentiment. Rather, it suggests memories all of us should have as we grow older, the kind we shall be needing, the older we grow.

This very fact emphasizes our keen interest in a thought-provoking story which concerns General Pickett when he was facing
the Union Army outside Richmond. The news of the birth of his
new baby had reached him. The Confederate lines were lighted
with bonfires, for the soldiers were rejoicing with their general.
The Union sentinels, calling across the space between the out-
posts, learned the explanation. They sent word to General Grant's
headquarters that the Confederates were celebrating the birth
of General Pickett's baby, word of whose arrival had just reached
the army. By order of General Grant fires were lighted in the
Federal lines to help the Confederates celebrate the birth of the
child, and the next day Union officers sent a graceful letter
through the lines, under a flag of truce, bearing to General
Pickett the congratulations of his enemies. In the note were words
of gracious salutation and of happy felicitations.

As Harry Emerson Fosdick has said, "That story lights up
a great truth." Contemplating the scene, we "see that what was
crazy there, mad, demented, execrable, was not the goodwill,
the care for a family, the love of a child. That was sensible. But
the hatred, the vindictiveness, the fratricidal strife—that was
insane." [2]

Fortunately, sane people do eventually learn what is really
important in their relationships. Some require a longer time than
others, but there are experiences that make us frankly face the
fact that first things must always be put first—or we ourselves are
lost.

IV. Spiritual Safety

We are making up our minds now as to what we believe is
spiritually important. It is not a question as to whether we should;
we are compelled to decide. Daily we reach decisions with regard
to our faith—or lack of it. At the same time, we are helping to

[2] *What Is Vital in Religion* (New York, Harper and Brothers, 1955), p.
41. Used by permission.

make up the minds of other people in the world. It does not matter whether we refer to spiritual security or "salvation" or not. The vital issue has to do with our eternal safety.

Nationally we are forced to face what this means. Roger Babson has emphasized that there is now no escaping the facts. He refers to those students who came from China a generation ago to continue their education in this country. Some of them had government scholarships. In a special newsletter, on February 21, 1955, Mr. Babson writes: As these young people "matured and became acquainted with the way our businessmen and politicians acted, they truly wondered if we were a Christian nation." [3]

Referring to the thousands who had come to universities in New York, Chicago, and other American cities, for their postgraduate work, he states that obviously they concluded that we in America were hypocrites. They returned to China declaring that, as far as we are concerned, the Bible is a forgotten book. They said that our missionaries did not truly represent America. This suggests how the Russian Communists could later convince the Chinese that our religious emissaries were using our Bibles only to put them, the Chinese, asleep while we robbed their country.

Whether we agree with this assertion of Roger Babson or not, his statement provokes the most earnest thinking. We are forced to face what we consider to be of supreme importance, what is really vital for our nation.

Consider the statement of a congressman with whom Dr. Ray Anderson was having lunch one day. The former Moderator of the United Presbyterian Church, U.S.A., asked this political leader what he considered our hope for civilization. The man replied that religion was of course our one hope. Christianity, he declared, offers us the way out. He went on vividly to describe what he believed about the vital significance of spiritual resources.

[3] Used by permission.

After a while, Dr. Anderson turned quietly to his comrade, and asked, "And do you attend the services of the Church?" With embarrassment that was painfully disturbing, the congressman hurriedly tried to explain that he was so busy with political affairs that he scarcely had time to worship on Sunday.

His first statement did not represent what he really thought was important. His deeds clearly did. Our lips may tell, or fail to tell, what we consider of supreme importance. All of us constantly proclaim our belief with our lives.

Voltaire did not deny this, even when he refused to accept Christianity. A friend observed him as he bared his head while the crucifix was carried past him during a religious procession. Turning to the agnostic, the friend remarked, "I did not know you were on speaking terms with God." The reply of Voltaire was, "We salute, but we do not speak." Far more than a salutation to God is necessary, however, if we are ever to understand the eternally vital importance of Christianity. Moreover, some decision relevant to this is inescapable.

This is pinpointed in each individual's experience. It is what a young colonel learned, not too long before I met him. He explained it quite simply, as we were talking in a Western city of the difficulties and dangers of our contemporary life which are exaggerated by our almost unbelievable advances in science. This young officer had been assigned to one of the sand flats where A-bomb tests were being made. Approximately six months earlier, he had united with the Church. Sensing the relationship of the so-called advances of science to the imperative necessity of some satisfactory solution, which science can never offer, he felt compelled to emphasize his conclusions. As we stood together one day in the church, of which he is a member, he pointed toward the front of the sanctuary. We were where both of us could clearly see the altar and the cross beyond. Almost in a whisper, he said, "There is our hope—the one thing of supreme importance."

Once we expected evangelists frequently, even glibly, to refer to the cross, as they quoted and discussed the text "What shall I do to inherit eternal life?" Now everyone with intelligence is using the same idea—whether the adjective *eternal* is included or deleted.

Many of us may not be employing the precise language of the young ruler, when he confessed the tension he felt so keenly. Nevertheless, we are raising the same interrogation. Sometimes the idea is presented thus: *How in the name of reason can we escape complete annihilation?*

The question "What is really important?" comes in *some* form to all of us. Each of us must try to answer it. It always involves an awareness of God Himself—if we understand its deepest significance.

No wonder Leslie Weatherhead refers sadly to an elderly gentleman—past eighty—who asked him for a conference. At the time, the older man was frightened because of approaching death. When Dr. Weatherhead asked whether he attended the services of the Church, the frightened individual replied: "I have led a very busy life. I have not had time for that." Doing a little quick mathematical figuring, the minister realized that if this man, now frightened at death, had even given his thoughts to great spiritual truths on Sunday only, he would have had four thousand such days with which to deal with matters of eternal consequence. By his own confession—"I have not had time for that"—he had been too busy for God!

Fortunately, there are those who have discovered what is of supreme importance. They have not merely realized that God must be given priority, but that He is indispensable—both for themselves and for all other people. When William Rainey Harper, at one time president of the University of Chicago, and world-famous Hebrew scholar, neared the end of his physical life, he sent for Dr. Frank Gunsaulus, the well-known Congregational minister of Chicago. Turning to this ministerial friend, after he was seated by him, President Harper made a simple request: "Frank, pray with me, 'Now I lay me down to sleep.'"

Jesus himself, when he came to the conclusion of his earthly career, dying on the cross, reverently prayed, "Father, into Thy hands I commend my spirit."

There is nothing more important for any of us today, or for our world, than to give ourselves to God, as we say with complete sincerity, "Father, into Thy hands I commend my spirit."

SUMMARY

Today we are deciding whether our lives will be:
A masterpiece, a mixture, or a mess.

I. **Physical safety itself depends upon the care with which**
1. We drive our cars and handle transportation of all kinds.
2. It depends upon our refusing to risk life for a trifle, or to
3. Emphasize speed as of more value than destination.
4. The *good of life* is more important than *goods in life.*

II. **Mental satisfaction is the result of our seeing**
1. "The things that are more excellent," and realizing
2. That a birthright is of more worth than food;
3. That radioactive fallout is more significant than "fallout" at a dance.

III. **Social security is more vital than we readily confess.**
1. Freedom of speech is a treasure we dare not lose.
2. Concern for all people is essential for personal welfare.
3. All social relationships, such as the home and the church, are vitally

Relevant to happiness that abides.

IV. **Spiritual safety is of eternal consequence for each of us.**
1. We are now nationally involved in a conflict with atheism and secularism.
2. Politics must be made Christian if we are to have the advantages of a Christian society.

3. The individual is still the key to the door that opens
   Into a blessed social order.

4. Awareness of God, and an eager response to Him, are
   indispensable

   If we are to enjoy a blessed tomorrow, as well as eternal
   life today.

III

What We Need Most

"He knew all the little answers, but never asked the big questions." This embarrassing statement, made in *Point of No Return*, disturbs all of us who are eager to understand life. For with painful accuracy the author, Marquand, is describing too many of us. That is why I raise this question, Do we know what we need most? Obviously it is one of the most serious inquiries anyone can try to answer.

Pondering these words, some of us may recall how frequently people have asked, "What are your needs?" with respect to things which were not vital to our deepest satisfaction. Since the days of Athens, tradesmen of various countries have used the same words. In a friendly way, sales people still ask us about our needs. It may be at the store, at the office, or in some industrial plant where men are concerned with the problem of rapid turnover.

But the question I am raising is much deeper and far more significant. It concerns our *deepest needs*. Unless we discover these, we miss life itself.

Paul must have been thinking of the importance of this vital truth when he wrote: "And the peace of God, which passeth all understanding, shall keep your hearts and minds through Christ Jesus" (Philippians 4:7).

I. The Peace of God

Most of us know we must have peace—if life ever brings us blessedness. We are hearing so much of "peace of mind," however, that many people are confused in their thinking with reference to what is really essential. "Always looking for a faster, easier way to do things, Americans are now trying to buy peace of mind at the corner drugstore." Writing this sentence in *Family Week* some time ago, Jack Glasner was referring to tranquilizing drugs. But he is also dealing with a basic truth; namely, that there is no monetary price tag on inner peace. It is not like a bottle of milk left on our doorstep while we are asleep. It cannot be wrapped in a cellophane package and carried home in our pocket.

1. Indeed, if we are intelligently to seek peace we must learn where we can find it, in order to understand what it is. That means, of course, that if we are to avoid looking in the wrong place we must know *what it is not*.

(1) Peace is certainly not placidity; it is not tranquillity. All too often, if we are fortunate enough to find inward calm it is in the midst of turmoil. There are those, indeed, who have been forced to seek peace while they were fighting. The letter which a soldier wrote to his wife, during World War II, as a result of receiving many irritating letters from her is more than suggestive. "For goodness' sakes," he earnestly appealed, "let me fight this war in peace!"

We may smile at this, but it vividly suggests how some of us must experience peace in the midst of trouble, turmoil, and conflict if we are ever to discover it. Obviously, peace can never be mere placidity.

(2) *Nor is peace contentment.* If it were, many cows would

be more blessed than human beings can ever hope to become. There may be those who pray for contentment, feeling as did Walt Whitman, on certain occasions, when he praised animals for avoiding the disturbance of a conscience. Recall how he commended cows because they did not ever worry over their troubles or failures or sins. Even if it were possible for all of us to become cows, manifestly we would descend to a low level of prayer by appealing for a state which only the lower animals enjoy. This is clearly not the peace of God of which Paul is writing.

(3) *Certainly this peace does not mean that we are to be left alone.* That would mean irresponsibility. The attitude indicated by this term is the opposite of Godlikeness. There are times when we may feel that it would be good to make our own the words of the Ancient Mariner, "Alone; alone on a wide, wide sea." In our finer hours, however, we know that even if we were physically alone we could not completely avoid a sense of responsibility and obligation.

(4) *Obviously the peace of God does not mean escape from life.* Jesus never did try to run away from life. He did not retreat to a monastery. Rather he lived at the very center of things in the Palestine of his day. He made it quite plain that he had come that we "might have life." It was, indeed, because he knew inner calm that he exclaimed: "Peace I leave with you, my peace I give unto you: not as the world giveth, give I unto you. Let not your heart be troubled, neither let it be afraid" (John 14:27).

Among other critics Jesus is answering are those who confuse *feeling* with *fact*. To *be* good is far more important than to *feel* good. This he made quite plain.

2. If the peace of God fits none of the descriptions indicated, what then is it? Certainly it is not the result of a mere mental state, as important as this may be. Indeed, strange as it may sound to some, *peace of mind* is not equivalent to *peace of God*. What Paul is describing in his letter to the Philippians is not dependent upon any outward circumstances. Conditions may change in char-

acter, but not God! Too many of us want peace of mind without the *mind of peace*, that is, a mind committed to the purposes of peace. We want peace of mind without the God of peace—the One who alone can guarantee it. The very clarity of St. Paul's vivid style of writing has, strangely enough, made it easy for many to miss his message.

"The peace of God, which passeth all understanding," does not, fortunately, surpass our experience, and therefore the possibility of each of us claiming it. The peace of God is for everybody, or it would not be a Godlike gift and another proof of divine grace.

Certainly only so long as God has the central place in our minds and "streams through" us "to other people" can we experience true peace. Many of us readily agree with W. E. Sangster, therefore, when he declares: "God can only stay in you when He passes through you." To covet Him, as the same writer adds, for what we are to get out of Him "is blasphemous and contradictory in its very theme." [1]

3. How, then, are we to seek this peace? The almost abrupt answer is that we are never to seek it for itself. Like happiness, this is a by-product of character—a specific kind of character—namely, one that is Christian. No one will ever find peace that abides by seeking it. *We find it only when we seek the God who alone can give it.*

(1) This means committing ourselves to the will of God, to His divine purpose. Listen again to Christ: "Peace I leave with you, my peace I give unto you: not as the world giveth, give I unto you. Let not your heart be troubled, neither let it be afraid" (John 14:27). His is not the popular method of procedure, because it is divinely different.

(2) As we follow in his path to peace, we appreciate more than ever what Hugh Walpole emphasized when he coined the

[1] *The Secret of Radiant Life* (Nashville, Tenn., Abingdon Press, 1957), p. 55.

word *serendipity*. Historically the term refers to three princes of
Serendip, an island south of India now called Ceylon. Accord-
ing to an ancient legend, every time these princes of Serendip
sought something the unexpected happened. When they looked
for one thing, apparently by coincidence they found valuables for
which they were not seeking.

Many individuals since then have demonstrated that they,
too, have made wonderful discoveries altogether unintentionally.
There was Columbus, looking for a new route to the Far East,
when, as Emerson reminds us, he "stubbed his toe" on America.
Edison was searching for an electric light when he found the
phonograph. Look, too, at that chemist holding a test tube over
a fire with a few grains of rice in it. He happens to drop the test
tube. Picking it up, he discovers that the rice grains have ex-
ploded. And there is puffed rice!

(3) It is not irreverent to say that the peace of God comes
to us in a way not altogether different. It becomes ours when God
gives Himself to us. We find it when we discover the Heavenly
Father. Peace is the result of Christian prayer, and prayer in its
highest experience is partaking of, and participating in, Reality.

As this becomes our personal experience, we understand why
Dr. David Fink declares, "Man's darkest continent is the human
mind." What this physician means is that our own mind is the
darkest area of human personality. When we accept God, we do
not merely see this truth, in divine light, but at the same moment
we receive this gift: Peace!

4. *Thus prayer leads us to peace,* because prayer means
"joining reality." It is accepting the peace of God, as a gift from
Him, for whom, in our wisest moments, we long more ardently
than for any gift we may receive from Him.

Indeed, Christianity is saying "yes" to God. That means saying, "Yes, there is a God," and saying "yes" to this God. For He
is of supreme worth, more "valuable" than all other offerings or
gifts we can receive.

A student of music finally gained insight into this vital principle, after becoming interested in Mozart. At first, however, he kept saying, "I, I, I," even when he discussed the music of Mozart. After a while he learned to say, "I and Mozart." Following years of discipline and training, he referred to his avocation by saying, "Mozart and I." At long last, fortunately, he learned the power and force of great music. Then he said, quite simply but very earnestly, "Mozart!"

II. The Power of God

What makes this peace of God so meaningful is the fact that it is the gift of One whose power is in harmony with His character. Furthermore, this capacity for *giving* and *keeping* is available for us. This explains why Paul used such a strong verb when he wrote: ". . . *shall keep your hearts and minds through Christ Jesus.*"

1. Recall how some have referred to their awareness of this power. Many Biblical writers have written vividly of their experiences. "I lift up my eyes to the hills. From whence does my help come? My help comes from the Lord, who made heaven and earth" (Psalm 121:1, 2, RSV). It was probably another writer who with confidence affirmed: "God is our refuge and strength, a very present help in trouble" (Psalm 46:1, KJV).

The author of the Twenty-third Psalm certainly was sure of the resources of God. Eagerly and happily he exclaimed: "Yea, though I walk through the valley of the shadow of death, I will fear no evil" (Psalm 23:4, KJV). So, "Our God is able," is not merely the testimony of a small group of men whose story is told in the book of Daniel; it is the affirmation of all who have found in God power to keep the peace which He brings.

Alone, we are simply not capable of meeting life's exacting demands. But our divine Friend has the necessary strength. An old East End woman of London brought this dramatically to the attention of Muriel Lester, dedicated social worker of Kingsley

Hall. Charged with breaking her promises and doing wrong, this old woman declared first she was innocent. When evidence of her failures was forthcoming, she began to weep. Sobbing through her tears, she exclaimed: "Oh, Miss! I'm as good a woman as God ever made . . . only I can't live up to it." Neither can we—without divine aid!

That is the reason we keep hearing so much of God's presence as we turn the pages of the New Testament. The truth becomes clear and appealing. "God is a Spirit: and they that worship him must worship him in spirit and in truth" (John 4:24). "If ye love me, keep my commandments. And I will pray the Father, and he shall give you another Comforter, that he may abide with you forever" (John 14:15, 16). No wonder a New Testament writer was happy to reaffirm the faith of one of his own contemporaries: "In him we live, and move, and have our being" (Acts 17:28). So another excitedly exclaimed, "God is love" (I John 4:8).

2. Whether we believe in God's power or whether we think it is available for us, in our discerning moments we certainly are aware of our need for it. Again and again we face dangers and difficulties which not merely rob us of our peace of mind but which also upset us emotionally when we doubt that there are adequate resources for us.

Whoever we are, wherever we live, we must face, and finally feel most keenly, the need for resources with which to meet *guilt*, *grief*, and the *grave*.

Although many of us apparently do not want to confess this, eventually we must try to handle all of them. Some of us, indeed, may try to escape a great deal of grief by not loving deeply and understandingly. We realize that the more we love, the more certain it is that we will have to deal with grief. The larger the number of people for whom we care deeply, the more frequently we shall have to suffer—when they are pained. But even if we decide to love only ourselves, we do not escape the necessity of dealing with grief. For eventually we may feel so sorry for ourselves we can scarcely avoid weeping, although we refuse to go out and eat worms!

So, seeing life steadily and clearly, we are aware that we must handle guilt some way. Even though we may not like the term, the fact of which it speaks is inescapable. A conversation between a swimmer in one of the rivers of Florida and an acquaintance who was on the bank underscores this. "Are there any alligators in this river?" asked the man in the water. "No, not a single one," assured his friend who was standing near. The swimmer was still disturbed. Again he asked: "If there are no alligators, what are those gray forms I see? Are you sure there are no alligators?" "Certainly," replied this newly made friend who was standing on the bank. "There are no alligators down there. Those gray forms you see are sharks that have chased the alligators away." So, this problem of guilt remains, however we may refer to it.

We may know no more about its technical interpretations than did the student who thought neurosis and psychosis were two women to whom Paul sent his regards in his letter to the Romans. Whether we are ignorant spiritually, or otherwise, however, guilt is something we have to handle. Sooner or later we discover that, by ourselves, we are incapable of dealing with it adequately. We are forced to seek some power to help us.

No one of us can get rid of guilt by calling it by some other name. Handling it satisfactorily is not that easy. We still have to do something about it, however we describe it. The Christian philosophers—even more important, all Christians of great experience—show us the way. They assure us of the power of One who can handle the guilt that grieves and embarrasses us. Paul had this in mind when he wrote: "And the peace of God, which passeth all understanding, shall keep your hearts and minds through Christ Jesus" (Philippians 4:7, KJV).

Old age—and after that the grave! Both of these we must

also face—unless we die young. "Do you have anything to keep
me from getting old?" asked a girl at the corner drugstore. "Yes,"
replied the discerning druggist. "You can take your choice: arsenic
or rat poison!" The pharmacist was right. There is no way to
avoid old age and the grave—if we live long enough.

3. Fortunately, we can learn how to handle all these—grief,
guilt, and the grave—if we accept the power of God. His is the
force and the strength which can keep us, regardless of the conditions we face.

Consider St. Ignatius, Bishop of Antioch, who in the first
century after Christ was taken by Roman soldiers to the capital
of the Empire for execution. That did not rob him of the power
of God to sustain him. Under these circumstances he sends his
"heartiest greetings of pure joy" to the Christians of Ephesus.
His was a power with which he was not born. Nor had he created
it. Its reality, however, was one he could experience—and one he
therefore accepted.

Christianity emphasizes the inescapable importance of seeking those resources which God alone offers us. "Christianity is
strange," says Pascal; "it bids man recognize that he is vile, even
abominable, and yet bids him be like God. Without such a
counter-poise, this dignity would make him terribly vain, or this
humiliation would make him terribly abject." God alone offers us
the power by which we can avoid the sense of being vile and
abominable. Accepting divine resources, we are neither humili-
ated by defeat nor puffed up with the delusion and pride of having adequate strength of our own.

4. Contemporary conditions in our world emphasize more
forcefully than ever the necessity of our accepting divine power.
It is not merely something we desperately need; without it we
shall never have peace of mind—which is itself the gift of God.

We may never experience the unexpected deliverance of a
Simon Peter or a Paul, but whether we are young or old, we
need the strength of divine fellowship. To go on and on without

the power that can keep us only increases our fear. But with God, who can strengthen us, we dare to face today and tomorrow, regardless of what the future may bring.

III. Poise

It is only in this way that we gain poise for days of danger, despair, and apparent defeat. Whether we use the term *poise*, or some other word that indicates the same experience, we recognize a pronounced need. Indeed, it is far more difficult to cultivate "self-control" during the long, monotonous days of ordinary living than it is to guard against mistakes when we are aware of immediate "danger." It is no wonder that an ancient writer, who lived long before Jesus, wrote of gaining resources to walk on and on, without fainting, after he had already dealt with the "less exacting" accomplishment of being able to fly and run without becoming weary (Isaiah 40:31). All of us face the demands of daily duty which require divine reinforcement. They come through Christ Jesus.

1. Christ promises us that this can be our experience. So he says that his Father and he will come and live with us (John 14:23). Because Paul knew what this meant, he was always praying that "God would indwell" the hearts of his friends. Apropos of this, Dr. Adolf Diessmann, eminent authority on Paul, has counted the number of times Paul uses the expression "in Christ." He states that in the thirteen letters Paul may have written the phrase "in Christ" or "in him" or "in the Lord" occurs 164 times.[2] No wonder Paul could explain that "the peace of God . . . shall keep your hearts and minds through Christ Jesus (Philippians 4:7).

After all, it is the friend who is nearest us whom we believe, and from whom we receive personal help, who shows us the deeper meaning of poise. Realizing this, we eagerly make James Montgomery's words our own:

[2] *Paul* (New York, George H. Doran Co., 1926), p. 140.

> God is my strong salvation:
> What foe have I to fear?
> In darkness and temptation,
> My light, my help, is near:
> Though hosts encamp around me,
> Firm in the fight I stand;
> What terror can confound me,
> With God at my right hand?

Considering the vital relevancy of this experience, Charles Lamb said of Samuel Taylor Coleridge: "His great and dear spirit haunts me. I cannot think or make a criticism, without him."

2. This relationship between our deepest needs and the promise of Christ is not merely the point of contact but the point of departure for a clearer understanding of both religion and life. This is where and how we find the deeper meaning of faith. For, as St. John of the Cross so plainly says, faith "is the union of God with the soul." When we experience what this devoted follower of Christ describes, we learn that this trust ushers us immediately into the presence of God. He becomes our dear and intimate Comrade:

> 'Tis God's own peace within my soul
> Which forms my quiet mind.
> —ANONYMOUS

All this we discover and experience as the result of learning that the peace of God is always a vital personal experience of His divine love. These two—intimate love and the poise of divine peace—can never be separated. Whether we deal with divine compassion and concern by means of scholarly research, or in a very practical way, we quickly discover the relationship of love and peace. Agape, the Greek word for love which Paul made famous, does obviously refer to the absolute, as Paul Tillich points out, but it "adopts itself to relativities without losing the absolute." That is to say, divine love expresses itself in human understanding and concern for the welfare of people without losing its divinity. This is the glory of it.

3. No wonder the poise which we desperately need can be understood by any of us—if we really want to grasp its meaning. This is a most practical experience. Whether, however, we accept it or fail to receive it, sooner or later all of us reveal our desperate need for it.

A woman who had lost her husband, after he suffered with cancer, pointed this out sometime ago in an article in a popular magazine. The title of the widely read sketch, which later was published in book form, was "Death of a Man" (Lael Tucker Wertenbaker). Written out of the agony of learning of the malignancy, the article reveals intimacies which once would have been considered out of good taste. Let me emphasize, however, that I have no quarrel with the woman who described the sex life of husband and wife, the depth of despair which came to both of them, and even the painful desire for release by death. What is disturbing is that this daughter of a minister needed much more than human resources and something far more satisfying and strength-giving than human poise. In writing how her husband, attempting to kill himself, used fifteen "hypo" needles, and then finally slashed his wrists with a razor blade, she presents a dramatic scene which arrests our attention with painful but penetrating insight. The fear is real, and the need for poise is quite pronounced.

But see how Hugh Latimer readily confessed his fright, yet knew where to turn for help. "Pray for me!" he exclaims. "Sometimes I am so afraid I could creep into a mouse-hole." Accepting the divine aid of God, he was no coward when they bound him to the stake, and then burned him near Balliol college at Oxford.

If someone says the incident is too old and we do not now know how to accept God's help, let him consider a conversation between a group of friends during the last world war.

"That fellow always seems to be getting a kick out of life," a man remarked as he referred to an individual with a radiant personality who had entered the room.

"He does," replied a physician, and laughingly added, "What a fine liver he must have!"

"He has no worries. . . . I don't suppose he's got a boy at the war," commented another member of the group.

"He's probably having a very good time in business, making a pile," another said.

As these men talked, Dr. W. E. Sangster felt impelled to break in and share his knowledge with this statement: "Well, he has reasonably good health. But he is not making a pile! He's a schoolmaster. No! He has no boy at the war. In point of fact, he has three children. One is normal; one is deaf and dumb; and his only son is deaf, dumb, and an idiot. If you want to explain that man's fine quality of life, you must look elsewhere." [3]

Indeed, if we are ever to gain radiant poise under many conditions of life, we must look higher up! When everything seems to go against us, we need the resources of a Person greater than any individual near us—or of all people put together.

Thinking of the implications of this fact, A. E. Whitham once wrote: "So there seems to be more power in a tear on the cheek of God than in all the . . . tides that . . . pound our rocks to sand." There is, he adds, "more light in His compassionate smile than in the suns of a million summers, . . . more energy in this lever of the Cross than in the forces that hold the stars in their ways. The courtesy of God is the omnipotence of Heaven moving towards redemption. . . ." [4]

So, when we see Jesus expressing concern for the needs of men, women, and children, we eagerly recall his words: "He that hath seen me hath seen the Father" (John 14:9). Here we find power and poise: in the purpose and strength of a God like Christ.

[3] *The Secret of Radiant Life*, p. 16.
[4] *The Best of A. E. Whitham* (London, Epworth Press, 1954), p. 96.

SUMMARY

We shall have to ask the big questions,
If we expect important answers.

I. We need *peace*, but we must understand that:

1. This is the *peace of God*.

2. It is the result of *God's* pardon.

3. It is saying "Yes" to God.

II. We need *power*, but this, too, is God's gift.

1. We must have resources for handling:
Guilt, grief, and the grave.

2. "God is our refuge and strength."

3. "Round our restlessness flows His rest."

III. We need *poise*, that is, steady nerves.

1. This, too, is ours when God "indwells" us.

2. It is the result of our loving God
In Christ's spirit.

3. When we are wise, we pray daily:
"Father, into thy hands I commit my spirit."

IV

Wise Men Worship

"Glory to God in the highest, and on earth peace, good will toward men" (Luke 2:14). This anthem of praise thrills all of us who are Christians. Yet, as we ponder the advent stories in the Gospels of St. Luke and St. Matthew, the hymn of the "heavenly host" surprises us less than does the appearance of the Wise Men who came from afar to find the new king.

"Where is he that is born King of the Jews?" (Matthew 2:2) these men eagerly asked. The travelers from the East who had come to Jerusalem to worship one whose star they had been following were greatly excited. For many days—possibly for long weeks—some think for months—they had journeyed in the hope of finding the "King of the Jews." The story of Christ which they heard in Jerusalem confirmed their hopes, but hearing did not satisfy them. They had to see for themselves. Learning that Bethlehem was the town of which the prophets had written, they quickly departed, following again the star which "went before them." They would not end their journey or stop their search until they came to Mary with the young child.

I. Wonder That Is Curiosity Plus

There is something so deeply moving about the excitement of these men that no one of us can really begin to understand it until we recognize, in their attitude, the kind of wonder which possesses *all* wise men. Here is curiosity which has provoked great thinking. It is the kind that has constantly characterized scientists and saints—for all serious students of life are akin in their insatiable curiosity. They will not be satisfied with anything less than facts. Here, then, is wonder which is characterized by awe. It was their desire to know, and their reverence for, truth which made these searchers seek until they found.

It's not too much to say that, if we have active minds, we have curiosity akin to this. But the adjective *active* is the "catch"! It gives meaning to all mental development. No scientist ever discovers any significant truth until he is greatly moved by curiosity. This is the power that forces him to search for facts, and compels him to seek the answers to life's perplexing questions. It is, indeed, at the center of genuine desire. When we lose this, we surrender life itself.

This is obvious to anyone who stops to meditate on human existence. To lose interest in what has happened, and in what is now going on, means that we abandon the desire to live. It is, therefore, a serious mistake to refer condescendingly to the curiosity of children, suggesting thereby that this characteristic is one for the immature. Actually, it is a continuing attitude of the keenest-minded people we can ever know.

We glimpse this fact in some of the biographies carried in the English publication *Who's Who*, since each individual is asked to indicate his recreation. A writer, William Sansom, responded by saying that his recreation was "watching." This, of course, is not merely a good hobby or a rewarding avocation; it is serious business.

Most of the scientific discoveries have been made by people

who were watching. Harvey was looking at the veins and arteries in the body when he discovered the circulation of blood. Copernicus was gazing at the sky when he became convinced that the earth moved. Whether Newton was actually under a tree and looking at an apple that fell on him, when he announced the law of falling objects, is of secondary consequence. He was *somewhere*, and he was *watching*.

As a matter of fact, every creative genius has been impelled by curiosity. Think of the hundreds of efforts that Edison made before he gave us the incandescent lamp.

When we are too old to look for life's secrets, we are too old! Certain scholars—much too old—resented Jesus' affirmation that unless "you . . . become like children you will never enter the kingdom of heaven" (RSV). It was to the degree that they took exception to this declaration that they both misunderstood life and abandoned it. Although Huxley did not appreciate Jesus so much as we wish he had, this makes it all the more meaningful that he realized, as did Christ, that we must become as little children in the presence of truth—if we are ever to understand it. This is the spirit of true scientists everywhere.

We are no longer mentally keen when we lose our curiosity and abandon our search for truth or beauty or goodness or love— or any supreme value in life.

There is a spirit of wonder which deepens our *appreciation*, as it intensifies our eagerness to learn, when we marvel at anything. This was in Henry Vaughan's mind when he wrote that he "saw Eternity the other night like a great ring of pure and endless light." This insight made him add: "All [was as] calm as it was bright." So, too, Kingsley exclaims:

> See in every hedgerow
> Marks of angels' feet,
> Epics in each pebble
> Underneath our feet.[1]

[1] "The Invitation to Tom Hughes."

This kind of appreciation causes us to marvel at the beauty of a rose. That is how we gain high evaluation of its loveliness, and respond to beauty with keen personal appreciation. Wise people do not laugh at this attitude, for to abandon our sense of wonder means we lose understanding, not merely of beauty, but of other exciting experiences which challenge us.

We so feel the power of wonder we can understand these words:

> If of thy mortal goods thou art bereft,
> And from thy slender store two loaves alone to thee are left,
> Sell one, and with the dole
> Buy hyacinths to feed thy soul.[2]

Without such appreciation of life's best gifts, we do not merely miss beauty that our eyes can see; we miss that which has to do with the deepest meaning of life itself. Quite wisely, therefore, Mohammed insisted that if we have two loaves of bread, we should sell one and buy a rose.

We marvel at the Parthenon, one of the two perfect buildings in the world. We appreciate its beauty—its expressions of life. It reminds us of the years 460 to 429 B.C., when Pericles, the famous Athenian statesman, worked so diligently to make Athens the center of the arts as well as the most beautiful city in the world. He was able to create ". . . a political, artistic and intellectual culture which made Athens" the center both of education and of art, in the Mediterranean world, for which all cultured people now give thanks.

Standing in excitement and admiration before the awe-inspiring ruins of this ancient temple, we are reminded that there is not a single straight line in the columns of this building. Here is still a challenge for modern man.

So, too, the beauty of the Taj Mahal humbles and thrills all who see it. Like a dazzling gem, its loveliness of perfection steals

[2] *Gulistan* of Moslih Eddin Saadi (Persia), c. 1184–c. 1291.

into our souls. Such breath-taking beauty makes us reverent, as it awes us with wonder. If, indeed, we can gaze upon the Taj Mahal, the Parthenon, or any majestic structure, and not feel the thrill of beauty, we have already lost life, life that has to do with the loveliness of perfection and the perfection of loveliness.

True reverence, however, goes even further. It impels us to meditate as we seek untiringly for an understanding of it. Thus life has meaning, not merely in terms of length, but also because of our new grasp of its breadth, depth, and height.

This is how Bernard of Clairvaux sought and found meaning in our human existence. He placed over the door of his monastery cell this question: "Bernard, why are you here?" Each time he entered his little room, he pondered the reason for life.

As kindly as we try to deal with people who have not searched for the message of life, there are some occasions when we react as did Dorothy Sayers, who felt so keenly this unfairness that she was impelled to write: "The only letter I ever wanted to address to 'average people' was one that says—I do resent your being so ignorant, lazy and unintelligent. Why don't you take the trouble of finding out what is Christianity and what isn't?"

It is the importance of this insight that Ralph Barton, once one of America's most gifted artist-caricaturists, was able to see at long last. Beginning his career as a member of the staff of a Kansas City newspaper, he moved to New York and became a feature cartoonist of the *New Yorker*. He left a letter with the request that it be published after he had taken his own life. This is part of that letter:

"I have had few real difficulties. I have had, on the contrary, an exceptionally glamorous life, as life goes, and I have had more than my share of affection and appreciation. The most charming, intelligent and important people I have known have liked me, and the list of my enemies is very flattering to me. . . . I have run from wife to wife, from house to house and from country to country in a ridiculous effort to escape from myself. . . . No one is responsible for this [suicide] and no person dies except myself who doubts. I did it because I'm fed up with inventing devices for getting through twenty-four hours a day."

This testimony of Ralph Barton is a vivid and dramatic revelation of how complete exhaustion comes to anyone who has lost the thrill of living, and thus the inner resources we desperately need. They can be attained, however, and used by each of us. But they become ours only as we cultivate reverence for truth and humanity. To the degree that we revere truth do we discover the most important facts of human existence, and then reverence for their meaning.

Sooner or later, we learn that life is intriguing and exciting when a propelling purpose possesses us and when we seek the attainment of a noble objective. All of us have to decide whether we are engaged in a hopeless struggle, fighting for—or against— what we feel will ultimately defeat us, or whether there is some worthy aim that is in harmony with the plan of the universe. Satisfactory answers do come when we treat God's gift with enough reverence to seek its meaning in a spirit of prayer.

Long before Jesus was born, earnest-minded men asked ques- tions—and kept on their trek for facts—until their search for truth and for life brought them a sense of gratitude and holy awe. One of them wrote: "Wait on the Lord: be of good courage, and he shall strengthen thine heart." Another was so deeply moved by his meditation that he declared the Lord would restore his soul. Another wise man who stopped to ponder insisted that in quiet- ness and confidence we do find strength.

Recall the experience of that young Jew who went into the temple and was so awed by the presence of God that he ex- claimed: "Woe is me! for I am undone; because I am a man of unclean lips, and I dwell in the midst of a people of unclean lips: for mine eyes have seen the King, the Lord of hosts" (Isaiah 6:5, KJV). Later, wonder, gratitude, and grace made the same young man testify: "Thou dost keep him in perfect peace, whose mind is stayed on thee, because he trusts in thee" (Isaiah 26:3, RSV).

The men who followed the star of Bethlehem were wise enough not to be ashamed of their reverence. Indeed, they were so awed and moved by their wonder that the story of their journey is read with keen interest after nearly two thousand years have passed. Whether these men were astrologers is of secondary importance. Theirs was the beginning of the discovery of a new kind of goodness.

To be sure, even now this Godlike quality is far from realized. Obviously the world is not what it ought to be. Nevertheless, we may well ponder how much of its true greatness is vitally related to what occurred in Bethlehem more than nineteen hundred years ago. With the coming of Christ, a new process of liberation was begun. It concerned the minds, as well as the bodies, of men. It is still going on, because it was initiated in a way never witnessed before.

A new love for beauty was born in the hearts of people. Raphael and Michelangelo found subjects worthy of their art. Handel could compose his *Messiah*. Milton was inspired to pen his incomparable poems. Dante had a subject which could make him a master. Sculptors, painters, and poets were inspired both to discover and to create beauty. For the King of Beauty had been born! The wonder in men's minds and hearts opened new avenues of expression. It was this thrilling and awe-inspiring curiosity that brought the Wise Men across deserts and mountains to marvel at, and adore, the infant King.

II. Worship That Is Love

When they came to "the young child," whose birth had summoned them to make their long journey, these men were moved with a holy amazement. They fell down and worshiped. They rejoiced, "with exceeding great joy." They did not simply recognize greatness when they witnessed it, although this is always the result of clear thinking; they *responded* to it. That is why they presented gifts to the King: gold, frankincense, and myrrh. Their wonder had led them to an experience of high worship. They were ready to bow before truth, beauty, and love.

They had demonstrated again that, because God is constantly seeking to reveal Himself, we can become aware of Him. We are to think of His character as Jesus reveals it. As has been well said, the Holy Spirit can bring an ever-increasing revelation to those who seek to understand Jesus. Of course, it is only through the Spirit of love that we ever really learn any truth.

Thus when we learn from Jesus, and become like him, we do not merely avoid errors, including those of personal prejudices; we make our response to goodness a continuing experience. It must be, for the goodness of God is infinite. "Whatsoever things are honest . . . just . . . pure . . . lovely . . . think on these things" (Philippians 4:8).

We did just this one day when we were flying over the snow-covered Alps of Switzerland. Nearly everyone in the plane was trying to get a better view. Many of the passengers wanted pictures of those marvelous scenes made by the brilliant sun flashing on the tops of the mountains and down in the valley. Even more vividly do I recall how the faces of these individuals became radiant as they gazed upon such loveliness.

This suggests what can happen to every person who gratefully and steadfastly centers his thoughts upon the character of Christ. That is why some of us are eager to look long enough, and reverently enough, to learn how to worship. Wherever we do this, in cathedral, church, or parish house, we seek the reality of God.

Such experiences as these lead us to another exciting discovery; namely, that *only when we love can we live*. Instead of being *lost* in love, we *find* ourselves in love. Without it, indeed, we end in despair. Without it, we surrender all reason for living.

The hour may even come when we are mature enough to understand the strange paradox of Augustine: "O, happy guilt of mine! O marvelous defection that turned me to so great a Redeemer!" Although his was a different kind of testimony, Bernard of Clairvaux would not permit himself to miss the relevancy of this truth. "My God I love Thee," he exclaimed, "not because I hope for heaven thereby, nor yet because, if I love not, I must forever die."

When we find ourselves in this spirit, we may be so moved that we bow in reverence as we ponder the greatness and goodness of God. This means that eventually we shall be captivated by divine Grace.

Manifestly this is what happened to these men. They diligently sought the new King, and at last found him, because they had cultivated the humility of those who bow before truth, beauty, and love, wherever they discover it.

Some of us were thinking of this *sine qua non* of life—humble teachability—again, as we approached the Church in Bethlehem, which is built over the grotto in which tradition says Jesus was born. Coming into the sanctuary through a door which is only four feet high, we were reminded that those who enter this church—or the experience of which it is a symbol—are forced to bow.

When I first came to Bethlehem's Church of the Nativity in 1933, like most travelers who have visited this sacred place, I was deeply moved. Recently, however, it seems to me that I was thinking, more earnestly and, I hope, more understandingly than ever before, of the tremendous significance of humility. Manifestly, if we are ever to learn the message and meaning of Christ, reverence is not merely a helpful virtue; it is an indispensable requisite.

Even though we may never fully understand the Incarnation, most of us can see that it suggests *nothing less than the humility of the Divine*. Although we may grasp something of the awe-inspiring truth of "God in man," which is at the heart of the Christian Evangel, we can hope for God to bring us complete peace only as we bow in adoration before the Christ.

Certainly if good will ever reigns on earth, bringing blessedness to men everywhere, it must come to millions of individual minds and hearts. It can begin with people who seek fortunate relationships with their fellows. It is just that practical. There is no appreciation of the value of persons without reverent response to the worth of a human being as such.

Here is a dramatic incident from the life of Rabbi Cohen, of Texas, which points in the right direction. The Jewish leader did not sleep much one night because he was concentrating on how to help a refugee. In the morning he said to Mrs. Cohen: "You can pack my bag. I'm going to Washington." Since he had only time to catch the early-morning train, when the banks were closed, on the way to the station he borrowed $100 from a member of his congregation.

On arriving in Washington, he was pained to hear that officials in the Department of Labor still insisted that the case of Lemchuk, the refugee, was one of obvious illegal entry. The rabbi called upon his congressman, insisting that he wanted to see the President of the United States on a matter of life and death.

Although President Taft was kind and friendly, he told Rabbi Cohen that the case was clearly one for the Department; and, as he well knew, they had rendered a decision. Realizing that he had lost, the rabbi stood up to leave, and thanked the President for seeing him ahead of some other visitors. Sick at heart, the haggard countenance could not hide the fact that he was physically exhausted.

"I'm sorry this had to happen to you, Rabbi Cohen," President Taft said. "But allow me to say that I certainly admire the way you Jews help each other out—traveling all the way up here from Galveston, Texas, when a member of your faith is in trouble."

"Member of my faith! This man is not a Jew," Rabbi Cohen exclaimed. "He's a Greek Catholic."

The usual placid expression of President Taft changed to one of marked surprise. "You mean to say, you traveled all the way up here at your own expense to help out a Greek Catholic?"

"He's in trouble; they're going to deport him on the next ship, and he'll face a firing squad when he gets back to Russia. He's a human being, Mr. President; a human life is at stake. That's the way I see it."

"Sit down, Rabbi Cohen," said the President. "Wait just a minute." Mr. Taft rang for a secretary.

The President remained silent, until the man came in. "Take a telegram," he said. "It goes to the Chief Inspector of Immigration at Galveston. Say, 'Hold Lemchuk in Galveston and release in the custody of Rabbi Cohen on his return.' Say, 'They'll hear direct from the Department,'" added the President of the United States.[3]

Here is the beginning of true wisdom, for it is the portrayal of genuine kindness—that is, essential kinship with other people. Thus we see something that transcends race, nation, and every kind of group loyalty. It has the touch of the eternal.

III. Wisdom

This was the essential characteristic that made the men *wise* who sought Jesus. Because they were convinced of greatness they themselves could not explain, these men from the East were intelligent enough to *wonder* and *worship*. They bowed before Jesus because they were convinced that this King should live. Fearing Herod's evil intent to kill Jesus, they changed their plans and "departed into their own country another way."

So, now, our truest wisdom is not expressed essentially in our desire to know *where* Jesus was born, or in our wish to present

[3] Anne Nathan and Harry Cohen, *The Man Who Stayed in Texas* (New York, Whittlesey House, 1941), pp. 198–200.

him with material offerings, as commendatory as that might be. Rather it is manifested in our desire *to help him live*. This is how we find the purpose and power of life. "Apart from me you can do nothing at all" (John 15:5, Phillips). Yielding ourselves to him, we let him live in us.

After all, true wisdom is portrayed in praising God with the same purpose which pursued and possessed Christ. We, therefore, do much more than simply join in the singing of the multitude of the heavenly host, chanting, "Glory to God in the highest, and on earth peace, good will toward men" (Luke 2:14). We do this—and much more. Our truest wisdom is in worship that praises by accepting, and portraying, the character of Christ.

Thus, our task is not essentially to save the world, but to make it worth saving. This is a far greater and a much more difficult procedure. It is an assignment only God is capable of handling.

This experience of divine fellowship, we now see, is both a personal and a social one. It is the result of worship, which concerns God and His world. By its very nature, it affects every human relationship because it belongs to all areas of life. We shall never outgrow it.

This fact was presented a number of years ago by a dramatic incident in England's House of Parliament. One of the members, Mr. Clynes, was being sarcastically heckled and bitterly denounced by the opposition because he was insisting on the highest possible ethics in national relationships. Finally he was asked by a member of this distinguished body what their guiding principle in foreign relations should be. Mr. Clynes replied: "We haven't definitely formulated it, but I think we should base it on the Sermon on the Mount." The answer sounded so thoroughly naïve that an old admiral sprang to his feet and shouted, "Gentlemen, gentlemen, if you are going to base the foreign policy of the British Empire on the Sermon on the Mount, then all that I have to say is, 'God help England!'" Mr. Clynes' immediate reply was, "And He will!"

This is the truth we find difficult to accept. Yet it is at the very center of Christian faith. That explains why the "foolishness" of our religion is wiser than the wisdom of men. God is like Christ. This suggests the deep satisfaction of those who trust Him to demonstrate this.

Consider how this truth often comes in the form of a challenge which is intimately personal. George Adam Smith depicts it. He was traveling on a train in France between Calais and Paris, when he discovered that a traveling companion, for part of the journey, was a young priest of another church. During a friendly conversation this young man informed Sir George that he was on his way to the Belgian Congo. Prior to sailing, he was on his way to see his mother, "for the last time," as he put it. "But why the last time?" asked Sir George. "Because," said the priest, "the average lifetime of a missionary on the Congo is two and a half years." This was before conditions of health had been improved to the degree with which we are familiar today.

The train rolled into the station, and as the two men parted, Sir George asked his young friend, "But—why go?" Placing his hand on his heart, the youthful priest quietly said, "The life that I now live, I live by faith in him who loved me and gave himself for me." [4]

Although this occurred two generations ago, it dramatically underscores the Christian character of world-wide concern. In heroic lives such as this, the drama of the cross and the wisdom of worship, love, and praise are all reenacted. So vividly is the wisdom of this adoration presented in dedication that it demands a quality of service any of us can see and understand.

Wise spiritual insight such as this makes an ordinary man extraordinary. He becomes like eight men in one. Spending his life in ordinary endeavors, he executes his assignments in an extraordinary fashion. Here is wisdom and worship of both the

[4] F. W. Dillistone, *The Significance of the Cross* (Philadelphia, The Westminster Press, 1944), p. 224.

highest and holiest nature. Ultimately this can make us aware of God in our minds and hearts.

Although we may understand something of this awe-inspiring truth as we gaze on Christ, who is "God in man," we can never hope for the Divine to bring us real peace until we ourselves bow in sincere adoration before God. Certainly if good will ever reigns on earth, bringing peace, it must come to the millions of individual minds and hearts in our world.

Christ made this very plain. He believed, and taught, that God is on the side of the right. He declared that to the degree our love for truth, beauty, and goodness is portrayed in our human relationships, God is praised. Indeed, *our highest wisdom is in worshiping the Highest.* Our truest understanding of life is seen in our eagerness to know the divine will, to adore the Christlike God, and to demonstrate daily His character.

So, we are wise as we worship with hymns, with prayers and, most of all, with ardent devotion to the practical purposes of persons who are committed to, and endowed with, Christ's spirit. Thus do we find *LIFE*, spelled with capital letters.

SUMMARY

The men who came from "afar" in search of the "King of the Jews" show us the wisdom of worship.

I. **Like other wise men their wonder was characterized by curiosity.**

1. All wise people are mentally eager to know life's secrets.

2. So wonder often underscores appreciation of beauty, truth, and love.

3. It leads us toward an understanding of life.

4. The search for facts brings us gratitude for life and holy awe of it.

II. **Worship becomes love.**

1. Because God loves us enough to seek us, we can "find" Him.

2. Only as we accept God's love do we truly love.

3. This reverent adoration makes us humble.

4. This love, in worship, deepens our concern for the welfare of all people.

III. **Wisdom is the result of wonder and of worship.**

1. We are wise enough to love Christ.

2. We seek to help him love.

3. We learn how wise it is to live as one family, Because God is the Father of us all.

V

We Claim What Is Ours

"All things are yours" (I Corinthians 3:21). St. Paul's statement is one of the most astounding ever written. Dictating a letter to his friends at Corinth, this declaration obviously fell spontaneously from his lips, as he spoke to his amanuensis. To Paul, it was natural and logical.

Do not center on Apollos, or Cephas, or Paul, he insists. Be united in Christ, and then accept the best that each of these men can offer you. Do not glory in any person or anything which has caused, or which will create, a rift in your Christian fellowship. It is harmful to the cause of Christ; it is most unwise, as far as we personally are concerned.

St. Paul was unquestionably disturbed most of all about the harm being caused by needless divisions. But he also deplores the inevitable loss sustained by any person who emphasizes one good to the exclusion of other benefits from every possible source.

Indeed, this keen-minded religious leader finds himself entering an expansive realm of intellectual and spiritual truth. Once he has begun to speak, his words flow freely with the rapidity and enthusiasm of a discoverer of some new, rich treasure. Surely he has struck a mine of truth, filled with nuggets of fine gold. Not merely all men, he says, and not simply what they have that is worth possessing, but *all things* are yours—absolutely everything! *The world, life, death, things present, things to come—all are yours.* The words scintillate with brilliancy. They strike us with the force of facts we wish to accept. They startle and arrest our minds. They are so simple, but so searching: "All things are yours."

What is the man saying? What does he have in mind? To ask the question seems to find Paul answering it himself. He assures us that he means exactly what he says. We can almost see the positive look of confidence on the face of the writer. Certainly he has spoken plainly enough for us to realize that he means to include everything.

I. We Claim Our Daily Blessings

As a matter of fact, the best things in this life are ours—if we understand what is best. The air we breathe belongs to no one person. It is free for all. There is no life without it. It is ours. The caressing breezes, the refreshing rain, the bright sunshine—these belong to no one corporation, to no single group of people. Does the physical universe have anything to offer which is better than these gifts and what they represent?

Physicians tell us sunshine and fresh air are two of the finest therapies in the world. They are preventive medicines, too. "Blessed sun," cried Carlyle, "it is sent to all living, and the whole wealth of the Bank of England is not equal to one beam of it."

In an unanticipated way, Alexander the Great learned the validity of this truth. Full of the pride of recent triumphs, one day he came upon Diogenes, who was enjoying the glory of the noonday sun. The powerful ruler condescended to speak to the philosopher. The mighty Alexander wanted to know if there was anything that he could do for Diogenes. "Yes," was the reply,

"Alexander can step aside from between me and the sunshine." Diogenes was wise. The sunshine was more than Alexander could give any man, and far better than his most valuable possessions.

So we can enjoy the morning star—if we arise early enough! No man owns it. It is God's, and therefore ours.

Flying from Paris to Beirut during a clear night is a priceless privilege, leaving unforgettable memories. The stars, hanging like great gems in the sky, belong to those who claim them. Sometimes I wonder if the reason for so many more poems on the loveliness of the sunset is not a reflection on our laziness, which prevents our enjoying the sunrise. Nevertheless, *both* experiences belong to us.

Certainly we share the best gifts with one another because they are ours together. No one has a corner on the market of the best. It is impossible to buy even the "margin" on it. The music of a waterfall, the patter of rain on the roof, the experience of watching God "wash His world," the smell of new-mown hay, the beauty of clouds banked against the sky—all these belong to us.

> I learned it on the meadow path,
> I learned it on the mountain stairs,
> The best things any mortal hath
> Are those which every mortal shares.

II. We Accept the Gifts of All Teachers

The ordinary blessings of mankind belong to us. We quickly discern this fact. There are other possessions, however, that we can claim when we realize our heritage. Every world-famous teacher has endowed us with the wealth of knowledge. It is only necessary that we lay hold on, that we claim, all that has been left us.

In the intellectual world truth belongs to those who will seize it. Most of the walls which now separate any of us from mental treasures are erected by ourselves—not by someone else. There are no great thoughts, no celebrated discoveries which are of practical value, that are not ours, or may be made ours, under the right circumstances. The truths of life have been, and are being, recorded.

Books are accessible; knowledge is available for everyone. Each of us can make the finest use imaginable of the mental treasures of the ages. These riches are not hoarded; they are free. What a store of wealth belongs to us! No scientific changes in our world can alter this fact. They serve only to emphasize it.

When we think in national or international terms, the words of Paul are as apropos, and as fresh, as though they had been written today—that is, for those who exercise their capacity to understand. It is necessary, to be sure, so to study this truth that we appropriate it.

We know, for instance, that the best in any section of the country, or in any nation, may be appreciated by those whose minds and hearts have no barriers. Robert E. Lee belongs to America—indeed, he belongs to mankind. Abraham Lincoln does not belong to one state or to one section or to one country. He is as much the South's as he is the North's. He belongs to every nation of the world. No real citizen of North Carolina or of Alabama or of London or of Paris will lose the good and the great in Lincoln just because he happens not to be from the same area. We are not to reject any good man or any inspiring message. If we do, we are robbing ourselves. We are, indeed, depriving ourselves of priceless possessions when we refuse to accept any value which any individual offers us. There is good in every master teacher. We are to make that our very own. It all rightfully belongs to us.

The greatest, the wisest, and the best are ours. They are when we learn what *possession* means, and then claim our own. Socrates, Plato, and Aristotle, though Greeks, are ours. Luther and Goethe, though Germans, are ours. Paderewski and Kreisler, John Knox and John Wesley, Moses and Amos, St. John and St. Jude— they are all ours. We need but to understand the truth of which

St. Paul writes, and then accept it. Treasures are available to everyone of us—treasures that neither moth nor rust can corrupt and that repose where thieves cannot break through and steal.

III. Religious Truth Is Ours

Certainly the same assertion may be made with regard to religion. If Paul's words have any real significance, it is just here.

Partisanship or sectarianism is foolish. It is short-sighted. It results in unreasonable and unnecessary personal and social loss.

George Matheson reasoned that no one individual had the only entrée to heaven and divine comradeship. He is right. God speaks through great minds everywhere and through every heart devoted to truth. There are many doors which lead into the temple of worship, many entrances by which we can go up to pray in the spirit of sincere devotion.

Like the apostle's statement, this fact constitutes a sharp rebuke to narrow religious living. No one individual—be he scientist, philosopher, or theologian—has all the truth. No one has every advantage. Too many individuals are blessed with insights into life for us to restrict ourselves to a limited number. When you and I realize what we possess, we shall receive religious inspiration from every possible source.

Unfortunately, as J. B. Phillips reminds us, there are those who insist that we join them in cultivating parochial-mindedness. Some declare that if we shall only jump through their "particular hoop" or sign on their special dotted line, they will be kind enough to introduce us to God. If not, then there's no God for us. Quite pertinently this writer insists that if there is a God, He is "available for me and every other Tom, Dick, or Harry who wants Him."[1] Canon Phillips' language is neither too plain nor too strong.

[1] *Your God Is Too Small* (New York, The Macmillan Company, 1952), p. 37.

A well-known religious leader in India, Keshab Chandar Sen, says: "I do believe, and I must candidly say, that no Christian sect puts forth the genuine and full Christ as he was and as he is, but, in some cases, a mutilated, disfigured Christ, and, what is more shameful, in many cases, a counterfeit Christ." [2]

These words may hurt us; they should cut us to the quick. But Chandar Sen is plainly saying that each of us should have all of Christ—not a single interpretation of him.

We can see this when we are Christians. Only when we refuse to act like bigoted sectarians can we be sure to receive the glory and greatness of life. Otherwise we are pitiful little people, who look at the stars, thinking they are "denominational."

For those who are wise, every individual with a helpful interpretation of religion—upon which we can depend and which shows us how we can gain power for living like Christ—is our friend. New light, fresh meaning, unexpected impetus and inspiring encouragement—these are ours—no matter what their source.

Unfortunately, some people permit themselves to be tagged. They are liberals or progressives, modernists or fundamentalists, Barthians or existenialists. Paul would belong to none of these groups. He would claim the good in each of them. The wise Christian will follow the same pattern. He will claim every good in all religious organizations. Just so he will use the insights into the meaning of life offered by every religious teacher. He will absorb truth wherever he can discover it. He will make every possible expression of goodness and beauty his personal possession. Emerson does just this when he declares that he owns "the seven stars and the solar year"; that he accepts and uses Plato's brain and even the gracious spirit of Jesus Christ.

When we understand great religion, we learn the messages of any hymnal, which includes poems and music from every worthy source. As has been wisely suggested, intelligent editors

[2] H. E. Fosdick, *What Is Vital in Religion* (New York, Harper and Brothers, 1955), p. 124. Used by permission.

of church music choose such hymns as: "Lead, Kindly Light," by
a Roman Catholic; "Dear Lord and Father of Mankind," by a
Quaker; "Jesus, Lover of My Soul," by an early Methodist; and
"God of Grace and God of Glory," by a contemporary Baptist.

IV. We Use Our Spiritual Power

This suggests an even further depth to which Paul goes, for
the apostle refers to some things much more difficult to possess
than information or knowledge or right mental attitudes. Indeed,
as he plunges into a discussion of what is distinctively spiritual,
he still insists, "All things are yours."

Before we can apprehend what he means with reference to
these matters, it will be well for us to recall how we make anything our very own. For there is no need to talk about what belongs to us, unless we know how to gain possession of it. How,
then, do we come to appropriate anything?

In the first place, we know it cannot be said that anything
is acquired by any individual unless, in some way, he "lays hold"
of it. That means that the higher values must be received, accepted, made our own. We can never "possess" the so-called
intangible values of life unless we *appreciate* and *understand*
them. Indeed, we must make them a part of our inner life if we
are ever actually to possess them. The meaning and purpose of
any experience must be grasped mentally and spiritually before
we can make it our own. Then, and only then, does it become
part of our inner life.

A legal deed may not make one the owner of anything. We
must learn to use it, if we claim any possession. So, by means of
a spiritual grasp we take what is ours. This is the way to appropriate it. Here is Raphael's "Sistine Madonna." We look at it.
It is there, and we are looking at it, but is it ours? It depends.
We can merely glance at it, and thus get a blurred vision. That,
however, will not mean very much.

But we may also look with the eyes of the artist. Then we

begin to drink in the meaning of it all. With appreciation and understanding we take that marvelous vision to ourselves. Into our minds and souls it comes, painting itself upon the canvas of our memories. We open our heart, and welcome the masterpiece, with deep affection and thanksgiving. Its beauty is painted on the walls of our memories.

Then, and only then, do we begin to see its message. At least to some extent, we understand its purpose. Thus, love of the beautiful becomes a part of us. What a glorious thing it is. What a rich experience it becomes! No one can ever take it from us. It will always be part of us. It belongs to those higher treasures which are timeless. Thus do we make any real value our very own.

Philip impressed this way of receiving truth on the Ethiopian official on the road to Gaza, when he asked, "Understandest thou what thou readest?" It is a question we must raise with ourselves in regard to any great truth, any thrilling beauty, or any challenging goodness, if we hope ever to possess it, that is, to claim it for our very own.

We must have open minds and hearts, if we are really to lay hold on anything. All is ours, if we claim it in this way. Anything belongs to us to the degree that we understand it, see and spiritually grasp and receive it.

Poetry and music are ours to the degree that we enter into their meaning, know how to interpret these arts and skills, understand their message, and respond to their appeal. Whatever is yours or mine becomes ours as we let it become part of ourselves. Appreciation, understanding, response, and spiritual grasp guarantee true possession of any value.

When we realize this, we can increasingly enter into the deeper meaning of Paul's startling but glorious statement. He is no oratorical fanatic. He talks like a wise man. He has discovered a great and heavenly truth.

V. We Accept Life in Its Completeness

In the light of these facts, consider life itself. It, too, is intimately personal. It must, therefore, be spiritually understood if we are to enjoy it. Existence and life are not the same thing. The purpose of life must be grasped if we learn its message, and thus claim its deepest significance as our very own. If, indeed, life is ours, we must have the correct interpretation of it, properly esteem its value, and rightly use it. When we do this, we begin to live, because we understand *how* to live. There has never been a more satisfactory or meaningful experience than that of Jesus Christ. Here is life at its highest and best. Jesus knew how to use his possessions. When we learn his outlook and attitude, and cultivate his spirit, we are able to say that life is ours.

This explains why we must be united with beauty, goodness, truth—receive them into ourselves, bathe in them mentally, commit ourselves spiritually to them, and thus claim them as our own.

Thus when "things present and things to come" become ours, we follow the same sensible course. These obviously make up the experiences of life. With moral and spiritual insight, we interpret their meaning and evaluate their significance. We become learners, and knowledge, which comes, lingers to give us wisdom.

"But," someone exclaims, "you are taking in too much. Paul evidently lost control of himself. He substituted oratory for good judgment. For 'all things' means experiences of every kind, including the 'evil' ones. Surely no one has ever satisfactorily interpreted evil. It continues to be the perplexing problem of life. At this very moment we are in a quandary about it."

This critic could go even further. For there is much more that is relevant. Evil often seems to possess us. Can we actually *possess* and *use* it? Certainly we can use suffering to help us understand those who are afflicted with pain. As we study how Jesus dealt with these evil experiences which came to him, we

see that he literally forced them to yield good. Unnumbered followers of his, too, have extracted good from the very troubles
of life. They have refused to be conquered and enslaved by them.
They have made evils the serfs of life, and compelled them to
render service. From trials they have learned patience. From
weakness they have wrested strength. From troubles they have
laid up treasures—of kindness, understanding, and appreciation
of others in difficulties of their own.

"Bring whatever you please, and I will turn it into good,"
declared Epictetus. Paul put it this way: "To them that love God
all things work together for good."

Fanny Crosby, who became blind at six weeks of age, knew
this was possible. She once wrote: "I am the happiest soul living.
If I had not been deprived of my sight, I would never have received so good an education, nor have cultivated so fine a mem-
ory, nor have been able to do good to so many people."

Too many of us do not realize we need the light of heaven—
until darkness encompasses us; that we need comfort—until sorrow
meets us; and that God is our one hope—until despair defeats us.
Fortunately, however, we can force regrettable experiences to
become our slaves and serve us.

So, we can extract the concealed lesson from physical evil,
and make that ours. Discouragement, disappointment, and even
failure—all these we can use in such a way that they assist us in
personal development, spiritual progress, and growth of character.
Think of John Bunyan and his years in prison. Consider John
Knox and his unnumbered enemies. Ponder again the trials of
the writer of the words, "all things are yours." Recall his struggles,
the physical anguish he underwent during the years of his Christian experience. Then meditate prayerfully on Jesus Christ and
his cross!

VI. We Claim Death As a Friend

The late Professor W. Cosby Bell, a distinguished instructor
who taught in the Episcopal Theological Seminary of Alexandria,

Virginia, shows us how to follow this pattern of study. A group of students were once discussing the oft-quoted twenty-eighth verse of the eighth chapter of Romans, a passage Professor Bell insisted was literally true. "But, Professor," some of his students argued, "you don't believe that all things work together for good—all the pain and suffering and misery—do you?" Dr. Bell quietly replied, "The things in themselves may not be good, but *you can make them work together for good.*"

Then came that afternoon when Dr. Bell's wife was killed in an automobile accident. He himself was left crippled. Under these circumstances he sent for the president of the seminary, and directed him to "tell my students that Romans 8:28 still holds good." When he learned that he was dying, he received the announcement calmly. Part of the message he sent to his students was: "I've grown surer of God every year of my life. . . . I can see now that death is just the smallest thing. . . . There's no real break—God is there—and life—and all that really counts in life—goes on!" [3]

Professor Bell himself did not live much longer. On his tomb there are carved the words from Paul's letter to the Romans. Intimate friends knew they had long been etched on his mind and heart. He had actually learned how to possess and use evil. Now he was possessing death, not being crushed by it.

All things ours? Yes, the very experience men call death is! Death, as a part of life, becomes ours when we understand that *life is,* and that it *can not die.* Paul undoubtedly looked on the sword or ax of the Roman executioner as the instrument which, by one sharp blow, was to burst his fetters. The sword was his.

We do not belong to death, for no real harm can come to those who are good. Indeed, when these individuals put aside their mortal garments, they enter more completely into the abundant life. "Blessed be my Lord for our sister, the death of the body from whom no man escapeth," wrote St. Francis, as, worn out with physical toil and suffering, he drew near his end.

[3] *If a Man Die* (New York, Charles Scribner's Sons, 1934), p. 199.

"Blessed are they who are found walking by Thy most holy will, for the second death shall have no power to do them harm." Death opens the door of new and blessed experiences for every Christian.

All things are ours, if we are Christ's and Christ is ours, for we then have the understanding mind and the boundless, possessive spirit of Jesus Christ, our Master!

SUMMARY

I. **Many blessings are ours each day, such as,**
   Sunshine,
   Rain,
   Water to drink,
   Beauty about us.

II. **We can learn the lessons of great teachers:**
   1. Truth about our world,
   2. Understanding of the meaning of human existence.

III. **All religious truth is ours.**
   1. We rob ourselves when we become sectarian.
   2. We are unfair to Christ and ourselves—
      When we refuse any religious insight,
      Or any true interpretation of character.

IV. **By means of our spiritual talent:**
   1. We search for the meaning of life;
   2. We accept the gift of beauty, truth and love.

V. **So, we accept *life* in its completeness.**
   1. We rejoice in its blessings.
   2. We learn to extract good from evil.

VI. **We even claim death as a friend, for**
   We believe it opens the door of
   New and blessed experiences,
   For all who live in the spirit of Christ.

VI

We Know Where We Are Going

Marked success crowned the ministry of Christ, as he began to teach in Judaea. In an almost unparalleled way multitudes followed this new Teacher, crowding the highways to see him and be with him. Apparently the response was all that anyone could wish for.

Quite quickly, however, it became obvious that those who followed Jesus either misunderstood or ignored the most important things he said. Certainly the vast majority of them did not appreciate his highest appeal. Many wished for material advantages. Jesus was looked upon as a skilled physician or as a popular leader whose power, they hoped, would eventually prevail over their national enemies.

Sizing up the situation, Christ left Jerusalem early and went to Galilee. He evoked the same popularity there. Great crowds came to be fed and healed.

It was time for a decision. It became necessary to sift the crowds, to draw a dividing line. Thus Jesus began to speak of his spiritual purpose, announcing that he was the "Bread of Life." The effect was almost instantaneous. People declared he was an impractical dreamer. In large groups they turned away. Just as they had come in throngs, so they left.

Manifestly affected by this loss of support, yet remaining true to his supreme purpose, Jesus turned to his more intimate friends, and asked, "Will you also go away?" The pathos in his words still moves us. We are aware of a keen sorrow in his soul, too deep, indeed, for any of us fully to appreciate. It was then that Simon Peter exclaimed: "Suppose we leave; to whom shall we go?"

The cryptic summary is unavoidable: "Leaving you, where shall we turn?" He may not have understood everything he said, but he raised one of the most searching interrogations with which any of us can deal.

I. Possible Detours

This is the question all of us must ask. It was timely then; it is relevant now. It is eventually inescapable. If we do not follow Christ, what detour shall we take in life? The question flashes across the heavens like lightning, penetrating recesses of mind and heart.

1. Simon and those with him could have turned back to Judaism. So can we. But—in familiar, contemporary language—*so what?* The Torah and the commandments, with their major emphases are good—good, but insufficient. Law cannot do for us what we most need. The thousands of legal prescriptions written in Washington, London, Paris—or centuries ago in the Middle East—are futile to deliver us from failure or the sense of guilt that oppresses us.

By depicting what is wrong, law warns us of evil. That warning is in order. Our deepest need, however, is not consciousness *of* wrong; it is deliverance *from* wrong. This is made possible by what our Christian forefathers called grace. Indeed, long before the New Testament wise men were aware of something far more vital than codes and rules of life. One prophetic writer summarized it this way: "What doth the Lord require of thee, but to do justly, and to love mercy, and to walk humbly with thy God?" (Micah 6:8). But how can we meet such a challenge without divine help?

The incompleteness of Judaism itself points to its fulfillment in Christianity. If we turn to Moses, he sends us back to Christ, for, quite correctly, Jesus says, "He wrote and spoke of me." A brilliant young Jew felt the importance of this searching fact when he asked his rabbi what the Messiah would have that Jesus did not have.

2. Another possibility, if we abandon Christ, is, of course, to turn from *all* religion. There are those who have so completely revolted against any divine direction that they have moved rapidly toward atheism. So can we. It is still possible to turn to no-god. But what is the advantage? What do we gain? What is the sense in taking this course?

In atheism the highest being we know is man. There is nothing superior to him. All possibility of a deity is discarded. Yet, at our best, we desire something beyond, over, and above us. *The higher we climb spiritually, the more keenly we feel the need of something still higher.*

Although he did not call his teaching atheism, Auguste Comte had no place for God in his scheme of things. He tried to find satisfaction by suggesting humanity as the Grand Etre. Theoretically this abstraction may be slightly better than atheism. Actually, he found it so unsatisfactory and dangerous that he felt it necessary to make a woman an object of worship. But this failed to meet the deepest needs of those who thought clearly of humanity's highest aspirations.

"If there were not a deity," said Voltaire, "we would have to invent one." He is right. Denial of a deity brings only hopelessness, despair, and eventual ruin. When France threw off her religion, and accepted the idea of no-god, the effect was so terrible that, with feverish haste, Robespierre, the leader of the

Jacobins, endeavored to restore the recognition of God. He realized what devastating results were inevitable.

Any nation goes to pieces without God. Any individual does, too. All of us collapse without divine resources. Such will always be the case.

Thinking as seriously as you possibly can, as you consider whether there is any religion of abiding worth, ask yourself quite frankly: To whom shall I go if I turn away from Christ? To no divine being? Then there is no one to guide you and me—and our world. There is no Ruler, no Leader, no Being in charge of things. There is no one at the helm.

3. "But," you say, "there are other possible courses." So there are. Pantheism is open. That says God is all and all is God. There can be no personal deity, no God of intimate fellowship for our minds and hearts, for you and me. Will you turn to this interpretation of life? Most of us know life too well to be satisfied with this. There must be Someone who can *personally* answer the demands of our hearts, if we are ever to find abiding satisfaction. "As the hart panteth after the water brooks, so panteth my soul after thee, O God."

4. Agnosticism is, of course, still a possibility. That means we try to find satisfaction in what we *do not know.* Strangely enough, however, with many people this has become quite popular. Obviously, though, *there can be no refuge in dogmatic doubts.*

To be sure, at times agnosticism may suggest a reverent attitude. Actually, however, it is usually not very humble, in spite of the suggestion of ignorance. And lack of knowledge is never a very inspiring experience.

5. Multitudes, of course, turn to materialism when they leave Christ. It is just as hopeless as atheism. Ultimately it offers only despair. It says everything is of the earth, earthy. It asserts that there is no soul, no mind above the brain. A writer of the Jewish race tried it once. He was compelled to sum up the results in these words: "Vanity of vanities; all is vanity. What profit hath

a man of all his labour which he taketh under the sun? One generation passeth away, and another generation cometh. . . . The sun also ariseth, and the sun goeth down, and hasteth to his place where he arose. . . . the eye is not satisfied with seeing, nor the ear filled with hearing. The thing that hath been, it is that which shall be; and that which is done is that which shall be done. . . . I have seen all the works that are done under the sun; and, behold, all is vanity and vexation of spirit" (Ecclesiastes 1:2–5, 8–9, 14).

Anyone who considers material things as the sum total of reality cannot possibly have a buoyant outlook for the future. If there is nothing more than matter, we can understand why some people feel it is in order to "curse the day of birth." Sooner or later, we have to say with finality: "Earth to earth; dust to dust; ashes to ashes."

Yet, because mammon is still their god, multitudes are killing themselves, working under the strains of emotional pressure day after day, without any final reward other than the things we see and handle. As a result, more people than ever before are suffering nervous breakdowns. Certainly we ought to be "diligent in business," as well as "fervent in spirit." That does not mean, however, that our supreme interest should be centered in gadgets or gold.

Jesus told of a man who built more and bigger barns to hold his crops. He said, "Soul, take thine ease. There is much laid up for thee." Actually he was addressing his stomach! That is the part of himself his possessions could satisfy. Had that man been living today, he would not have wanted to join the Communist party, but he would have been quite familiar with its basic philosophy.

6. Science was once the Messiah, the Savior, of many. At least they worshiped at her shrine. Few do so any more. The scientists themselves know altogether too well the inadequacies of the facts they have discovered. Try saying this:

Science is my shepherd; I shall not want.
It maketh me to lie down in green pastures;
It leadeth me beside the still waters.
It restoreth my soul;
It leadeth me in the paths of righteousness for its name's sake.
Yea, though I walk through the valley of the shadow of death,
I will fear no evil: for science is with me;
Its rod and its staff they comfort me.

The power of science we understand. The facts we have learned, by means of scientific research, show us how we can destroy our world. Most of us understand that if we use the destructive forces already demonstrated, we will have no world in which to contemplate a future.

7. Probably the most crowded detour taken by those who turn from Christ is still the one that promises pleasure. Across the long centuries men and women have sought to find satisfaction in this blind alley. Millions are still seeking physical exhilarations, only to end in futility instead of fulfillment.

A coach-plater, of London, shows us what happens when we take this detour. Harold Begbie tells his story in *The Ordinary Man and the Extraordinary Thing*.[1] "When I was a young man," the coach-plater told Begbie, "I lived for one thing, and one thing only—Sport." This man did not believe that anything in the whole world was comparable to Sport. He gave his thought completely to this passion of his life. While he was at work, his mind was on boxing, rowing, and racing. As soon as he could get away from his work, he would go down to Hungerford Stairs and scull on the Thames till it was dark. Then he would go where he could see a bit of fighting, or where he himself could engage in a sparring match. After that he would go home, tumble into bed, without prayers, of course, and fall asleep dreaming of Sport.

One day when this young man was crossing over Blackfriars

---

[1] (London, Hodder and Stoughton, Ltd., 1912), p. 188 ff. Used by permission.

Bridge he nearly pitched himself over. In fact, he came as near to it as one could without committing suicide, for he had lost the wish to live. His gloom and wretchedness created an unbearable loneliness. So pronounced was this that he felt as if he were alone in the whole universe. This is what drove the youth "to the verge of despair."

So, too, Byron finally learned the hard way that he was mistaken when he wrote, with "cocky" confidence, "Life sparkles only at the brain." After following the detour of this idea, he was compelled to admit that his days were "in the yellow leaf." For him "the flowers and fruits of love" were gone. "The worm, the canker, and the grief" were his alone.

George Fox tried many similar detours. A. C. Bickley, his biographer, tells us that wherever the melancholy youth went, he was solitary and sad.

A youth of twenty, he was nevertheless conscious of the fact that he was searching for something he did not have. Clergymen "listened with unaffected tedium" to him and, as Carlyle reminds us, advised him to seek solutions of his doubts in the most superficial and shallow way imaginable. Fox, however, eventually discovered that to follow any of these directions would be like "dropping buckets into empty wells." And all the time he was "drawing nothing" out, he was growing older and older.

II. The Highway to Life

Because we cannot meet life buoyantly with this emptiness, there are at least times when all of us long for a God capable of helping us. If we leave Christ, where shall we find One that can satisfy us? This young Jew, who was not just *a* man, but *The Man*, not *a* God, but *God revealing Himself to us*, shows us what will satisfy us today and forever.

Many, like George Tyrrell, have tried to be rid of him. But often they have joined this disturbed individual, following the controversy with his ecclesiastical superiors, when he said: "How glad one would be to get out of it all! But there is that strange Man on His cross who drives me back again and again."

How often some of us feel like crying out, "What have I to do with Thee, Thou Jesus of Nazareth?" As we have frequently been reminded, there are always torments and tortures for us when we turn from him. Uneasiness, doubts, and fears sweep over us until we settle this momentous issue between ourselves and the eternal Christ.

"There is a good which transcends the will of the King and the will of the people and transcends my overwrought and wretched will." So writes Robert Raynolds in *The Quality of Quiros*.[2] Keep lifting this idea high enough, and we shall see why Simon Peter came to learn that there is a good which transcends all human will and which is the *summum bonum* of life. This is Christ.

1. Consider, then, who this Master was. His character and his influence in history portray him as *the authority in the field of religion and life*. He leads us down no blind alley, because he knows life. He understands where to go and what to do. He always speaks with confidence and challenge.

The preacher to whom Spurgeon referred as one who would have made a very good martyr because he was so dry he would burn well does not represent Christ—or his message. Jesus was always interesting, exciting, and appealing, because he dealt so vitally with life. So those people who live with him now speak thrillingly of him.

A burglar, who broke into an apartment house in one of our cities, understood something of this significance of Christ—although doubtless he could not have explained how or why. The thief had stolen some very valuable jewelry. Apparently he had left no trace of his identity. After a long investigation, the police seemed to be facing a blank wall. Then, suddenly, they found a clue. In the apartment they came upon *a single handprint*. On

2 (Indianapolis, Bobbs-Merrill and Company, 1955), p. 293.

the mantel was an alabaster bust of Christ. The burglar had entered the apartment through that room. Later, the police learned that as the burglar looked hastily about, his eyes fell upon the face of Jesus. Before he touched anything in the apartment, he had walked to the statue and turned its face to the wall, and only then went about his stealing. But in doing so he left a fingerprint upon our Lord. As Joseph Sizoo has reminded us, it is always so. *Life ever stands condemned or justified by the test of Jesus Christ.*

> But thee, but thee, O Sovereign Seer of Time,
>
> . . . .
>
> O all men's Comrade, Servant, King, or Priest,—
> O, what amiss may I forgive in thee,
> Jesus, Good Paragon, Thou Crystal Christ? [3]

2. But he is more. He is capable of handling every situation because of his moral equipment and the spiritual fiber of his very being. A man who wrote a letter to the *Saturday Review* some time ago did not see this. He complained because a former article had suggested that our supreme need today is Christianity. The critic insisted this religion did not face hard facts. Indeed, he declared Christianity is too tender for these tough times. It must be that he had listened to someone other than the New Testament writers! They found Christ was not merely tough enough to face every imaginable difficulty, but that he offers us strength for the journey of life.

3. The most unbelievable challenge with which he dares us is that we can increasingly become like him. So he says, "I call you friends," and adds, "Greater things than these shall ye do." At the close of many startling statements he made in the Sermon on the Mount, he declares that we are to be perfect as God is perfect. The least thing this means is that we are to be constantly comparing our characters with the divine nature of God, not

---

[3] Sidney Lanier, "The Crystal Christ," from *Masterpieces of Religious Verse* (New York, Harper and Brothers, 1958), p. 419.

merely because Christ challenges us to do so, but because He is the One who completely satisfies the deepest desires of our hearts.

He says, "I reveal God; God is like me." So he gives us a personal God, a Deity to whom all of us can go, and find courage and strength for life, as well as purpose and meaning for its journey.

Sir James Simpson, the discoverer of chloroform, said that the greatest discovery he ever made is, "That I have a Savior." No wonder, too, W. E. Gladstone, following years of experience as a statesman, told the world that after all his thinking and reading he had reached the conclusion that all men had to come to Jesus as children. Similarly, Sir Oliver Lodge exclaimed, "Although an agnostic in my younger days, by sheer scientific research I was driven to believe in Jesus Christ as the one real power and Savior of the world."

I've tried the broken cisterns, Lord,
But ah! the waters failed;
E'en as I stooped to drink they fled,
And mocked me as I wailed.
Now none but Christ can satisfy,
None other name for me.
There's *life*, and *peace*, and *lasting joy*,
Lord Jesus, found in thee.

SUMMARY

Like Simon Peter and his friends, if we turn from Christ

I. We must choose some other way.

1. We can go back to Judaism, but
   The Prophets send us back to search for the Messiah.

2. We can abandon all religion, but
   Atheism offers us no help.

3. We can become Pantheists, but
   If God is all, and all is God,
   We have no personal friend.

4. We can accept agnosticism, but
   Lack of knowledge is never an aid.

5. We can turn to things, but
   All of us want more than food, drink, and clothes.

6. We can make science our deity, but
   Science gives us power—not a person.

7. We can give ourselves to pleasure, but
   Eventually we find we are
   "Dropping buckets into empty wells."

II. Christ shows us the one way.

1. He knows religion and life.

2. His moral equipment and spiritual resources are adequate for life.

3. He is our friend who offers life and peace and friendship.

VII

If Our Homes Survive

Forget the A-bomb and the H-bomb. Unless we can save our homes, our Western world has no future, for no civilization has ever survived the disintegration of its home life. . . . This is the exhortation of Carle C. Zimmerman, Professor of Sociology at Harvard. The sentences accurately summarize an address he gave in Boston, which the Associated Press widely publicized.

Based on history, as this assertion is, it becomes deeply moving for serious-minded people. It focuses our attention on a familiar greeting of St. Paul: "the Church that is in their house" (Romans 16:5). Contemporary facts force us to face the deeper meaning of these words. This is not just a lovely phrase, enjoyed by some who are obsessed with sentimentality. Rather, it has to do with life that is real—and the kind of religion that is valid and necessary for every day and age. For if we lose an intimate, personal religious experience in our homes, they will fall apart. We are driven to ask, therefore, what the words of Paul imply and how we can make them come to life.

This is particularly significant when we recall that long be-

fore the followers of Christ constructed buildings known as
churches, they met in their homes for worship. Christians did
not erect sanctuaries for formal services until the third century,
but believers met, in small companies, for praise, study, and dedication in the first century.

Such thought-provoking facts clearly suggest that if we have
a church today—and tomorrow—it will be in our homes—and will
rest upon the foundations we build there. Wherever else we may
meet for organized, formal worship, there will be Christian homes
from which members of the family go, and to which they return
for security and fellowship.

I. Information

To deal with such vital issues emphasizes the need for information of a comprehensive nature. At least theoretically most
of us know that it will take our keenest intelligence to make the
home meaningful, much less save it.

Therefore, the indispensable requisite of love should be the
first consideration. If I say that love is necessary for any happy
home, you would doubtlessly agree. But what is the nature of this
essential requirement? Even when we interpret it as "intelligent
affection," we are aware that we must search further for the real
significance of this experience. Certainly, if there is a home in
which the church is possible, and Christianity is demonstrated,
it will come as the result of members of the family assuming their
responsibilities seriously. This requires our gaining adequate
knowledge of social and personal psychology, a reasonable and
religious interpretation of sex, and sufficient insight into the worth
of spiritual growth.

If church and home survive—and that manifestly includes
the church *in* our homes—there are physical adjustments which
are imperatively necessary. We shall never study to show our
homes as places of worship, unless we know enough about ourselves, that is, our own *bodies* and *minds* to gain insight into the
meaning of our lives.

This is not simply necessary, but possible, even for those who are not familiar with technical terms which describe the experience. For surely all of us, including those without a formal education, can see that when we spend more time selecting a *house in which* to live than we do in choosing the *person with whom* we are to live, we have no moral right to anticipate a happy home. So, when we give more attention to the purchase of some modern labor-saving device than we do to the selection of a church, we do not simply fail properly to evaluate our homes and our church; we indicate we are not greatly concerned with their survival.

For this very reason, the intelligence of the realist is indispensable in gaining needed knowledge. Indeed, one disturbing kind of ignorance we must now overcome is that of the sentimentalist, the romanticist. It is demonstrated in many so-called saintly individuals who are actually neither *saintly nor sensible*. Never having learned the art of giving religious character to sex, they spend much of their time making derogatory statements about young people who are trying to discover the meaning and worth of human life. So, plagued by ignorance which springs from warped or superficial consideration of the physical self, these people never learn what St. Paul had in mind when he exclaimed, "Know ye not that ye are the temples of the Holy Spirit?" The inevitable result is too obvious. There is no church in such homes, for only as we ourselves are temples of the Holy Spirit can our homes become houses of worship.

Thus, again we disclose wisdom when we deal seriously—not lightly, or casually—with vital issues involved in making our homes religious. We refuse to succumb to the temptation of insisting that the necessary principles relevant to happy homes are quite simple. This may be true. But when we say these principles are easy to apply, we are not merely unwise; we show that we are unequipped to deal with either the home or the church.

For instance, we may continue to shout loudly that love will save the home. But we must understand both *what* love means and *how* to demonstrate it. Affection itself must be guided by common sense, as well as by spiritual concern. In a home where there are three children of school age, a father who must get to work on time, a mother responsible for breakfast, and only one bathroom, there are obviously many practical problems posed which cannot be solved by writing about love romantically—especially at 8:00 A.M.

Related vitally to these problems is another exceedingly important question: How shall we *sustain* love? Human relationships are never simple. Whenever we suggest that they are, we disclose gross ignorance. We may know something of the *strategy* for building a blessed home, and yet be altogether unfamiliar with the *tactics* which represent a daily and necessary procedure. Indeed, the divine daring which gives us strength to construct a church in our homes reminds us that, as Theodore Reik has said, "Only the brave can struggle to love."

That is why the entire issue of *information* about homes is so practical. It involves reverent knowledge of sex—recognizing this as an essential human relationship which, tragically, the church has left too frequently to two classes of people: the ignorant and the morally warped. It necessitates our understanding human nature, so that we may deal sensibly, and not merely facetiously, with in-laws, as well as with other members of the family. We may even discover that some who are related to us by blood are less "kin" to us than many people whom we meet in store, school, or church. Certainly we shall begin to see the necessity of adjustments relevant to money and other so-called material matters, with which we have to deal as long as we are in this world.

All this becomes a personal venture for each member of the family. Indeed, appreciation of each other is never vague and general; it is intimate and individualistic at the very moment it involves others. The realization of this basic fact will direct us to *learn together*. To the degree we want to grow together both

as husband and wife, and as parents and children, we find happy
fellowship. If within our homes we learn to push back the hori-
zons of mind and heart, we shall discover that home does bring
blessedness. There is no other place in the world comparable
to it.

II. Imagination

Information, however, cannot accomplish this alone. It must
have the aid of *imagination,* if we are to preserve homes in which
the Christian Church can become a reality. This is the response
of mature love, and it is most exacting. It may even involve pain.
It always necessitates projecting ourselves in the experiences of
our fellows.

It is more than walking in the shoes of a comrade, though this
would be a truly great Christian achievement for most of us.
Nor is it enough to be able to say, as did an Old Testament
prophet, "I sat where they sat." We never really understand people until we are so interested in them, and so concerned about
them, that we learn to crawl into their skins. To feel what another
feels, to become pained with the troubles of others, is a high
price to pay for friendship, but it is the lowest we dare pay—as
Christians. That is why *imagination,* like *love,* is such a grossly
misunderstood word. It has to do with that high Christian experience which enables us to put ourselves in the places of our neighbors, even though this means self-chosen suffering.

The difficulty of cultivating this capacity is evident quite
early. Here are two children, a boy and a girl, of pre-school age.
The two are walking together. The little girl excitedly exclaims
to her companion: "Wouldn't you like to be a bird, and fly and
fly and fly, 'way up in the air?" "Naw," answers her young male
companion, "I'd like to be an elephant and squirt water through
my nose." There it is! The tremendous difference between the
sexes, at which we often smile, but which too frequently we do
not seriously try to understand. Too many of us are unwilling to

cultivate the ability to cross the sex line with imagination—an art which requires both intelligence and Christian character.

Lift this quickly to a much higher level, and see what it can mean when two people are older. Take a glance at the wife of Racine, who often quarreled with her famous author-husband because, she said, he did not pay attention to the currants in her garden. Yet she herself never was interested in the dramatic tragedies which Racine wrote for stage and study—the creative work which was the very life of his life.

This widespread lack of understanding and imagination we sense in the exclamatory prayer of Thomas Bracken, who begged God to enlighten us to see more clearly in order that we would judge less harshly where we "cannot see." So he implores the Deity to help us draw more closely together, enabling us truly to appreciate one another.

Without mutual understanding, we not merely have no justified hope for a church; we lose our homes, and often old age itself becomes tragic. Recall how this is depicted in the declining years of Tolstoy. He and Sophie, his wife, should have enjoyed serenity and peace. This was not to be, however, in spite of the fact that their children were many and that Tolstoy himself had become famous. His wife insisted she wanted to be the writer's helpmate. But she was so jealous of her husband that she read his mail, searched his papers, and bitterly attacked his friends. Finally she drove the old man from the house to die of pneumonia in a railway station. The "love" which made Sophie bear Tolstoy many children was not adequate. She lacked understanding and insight—fortunate characteristics of those with imagination.

With reference to the same basic truth, it may not be too much to assert that if Vincent Van Gogh had been understood, he would never have lost his mental balance. Few people, however, seemed to care enough to try to appreciate this strange young genius. Although his earliest work was in the area of painting, Vincent's fundamental honesty kept him from joining in the organized fraud of art dealers. Many in this business could not understand such a man.

Falling in love with his London landlady's daughter, Ursula, Vincent proposed to her, but was rejected. He then became so depressed he returned to be with his family in Holland. After a second rejection, during another stay in London, this depressed youth returned to Paris on May 15, 1875. Seeking relief from his disappointment in love, he read the Bible constantly and turned toward a kind of fanatical mysticism. He went to many places of worship, including synagogues. He tried to earn a living as an assistant schoolmaster at Ramsgate, in England, and then as a lay preacher under the Methodist pastor at Isleworth. Discovering the wretched condition of the urban laboring classes, his sympathy went out to them. Later, on May 8, 1877, he left for Amsterdam to prepare himself to enter theology. After fourteen months he was compelled to give this up.

His father, though a pastor himself, had limited intelligence. He simply did not know what to do with a son like Vincent, who could not learn a trade and apparently refused to be taught anything else. Weary of argument, the Reverend Mr. Van Gogh had his son enrolled for a three-month course at a school for evangelists at Brussels. Without waiting for an appointment, Vincent left in December for the Borinage district of Belgium, eager to reveal the light of the Gospel to those who seemed to need it most, miners who were in extreme poverty.

He gave himself freely, teaching the children, tending the sick, and distributing his scanty means to the poor. But the consolation and faith he tried so eagerly to bring was not welcomed. All his efforts met with rebuff. He was not able to communicate with these people. He went to the extreme of blackening his face, in order to look like the miners. But he remained only a stranger. The Protestant leaders themselves did not understand him.

This is the beginning of a career of which the world would not even know, save for the fact that Vincent Van Gogh became one of its great artists. He died on July 29, 1890, at thirty-seven, misunderstood by most people, a saddened and broken man.[1]

This tragic character reminds us of the pronounced differences of individuals. In order to understand the distinctive characteristics of others, we must have the ability to put ourselves in their place. This makes it possible to appreciate those about us. Only with this eagerness to "hear" the unspoken desires of our family, can we hope for a home in which religion is healthy and strong. Without such homes, eventually we lose love of life itself, for all of us want friends who sincerely care for us.

This relationship demands the finest thinking of which we are capable, as well as the deepest feelings of our hearts. It is manifestly expensive, for it involves an understanding which goes far beyond curiosity about our acquaintances, or a superior air of condescension toward our fellows. We do not easily fathom the depths of even our friends' intellects. No wonder a young man was rebuked severely when he declared, in the presence of a brilliant girl, "Yes, I can read your thoughts." "Then," replied the young woman, "I beg your pardon!"

Only those who cultivate the ability to appreciate others can possibly develop the capacity to understand them. In our homes the desire for this capacity is of supreme importance. It is a requisite for blessedness.

All this is vitally relevant to what Samuel Kling underscores when he declares that the familiar terms *desertion* and *adultery* are "mere technicalities used to cast a smoke screen over the real causes" for divorce. The true explanations, this well-known divorce lawyer points out, are such faults in husbands as: *selfishness, lack of consideration in marriage relationships, untruthfulness, and lack of demonstrativeness.* In wives he sees the real reasons for misunderstanding and antipathy in faults like *nagging, frigidity, lack of consideration, slovenliness.*

[1] *Van Gogh,* by Frank Elgar (New York, Frederick A. Praeger, Inc., 1958), pp. 18 ff. Used by permission.

Although we may smile when we listen to a certain woman who was obviously lacking in sincere love, she throws light on this fundamental matter by a statement made confidentially to her beauty operator. "I've had my worries," asserted this lady, as she sat drying her hair under the lamp, "and sometimes I wonder if my husband has not grown tired of me." "What makes you say that?" asked her beauty expert. "Well, he hasn't been home in three years."

If this sounds ridiculously superficial, and even silly, I remind you that there are thousands of men and women who return day after day to their *residences,* but who have not been *home* for years. We can hardly hope to have a church in a home where this spirit prevails. It does not bring a happy glow, much less the presence of the Holy Spirit.

Only the imaginative can build a home in which the Christian Church can come to reality. This is because learning another person, that is, getting to know one, takes time, patience, and sympathetic concern. But it is worth everything it costs, for, to use a phrase of Dorothy Gardiner, this fellowship always includes *"the ecstasy of being understood."* This is vitally relevant to St. Paul's affirmation that we "are one body in Christ, and individually members one of another" (Romans 12:5). Devotion to God and aspiration to know and love Him require concern for, and appreciation of, all God's children—those in our homes as well as those outside.

III. Inspiration

Imagination can lead us a step further. It transforms monotony into *inspiration.* By means of it we cultivate blessed fellowship—the kind in which the spirit of Christ is *at home.* This is not unsophisticated sentimentality or unanalyzed romanticism. Rather, it has to do with the *creative endeavors of the whole family.*

It concerns the pursuits of the arts: music, drama, literature, writing—all possible contributions to worthy purposes. For every member of any happy home has some worthy interest. This is the practical portrayal of both aspiration and inspiration. Carlyle stated it this way: "Produce! In God's name, produce, if it be but the infinitesimalest fraction of a second!" We could not expect many to write as vividly and effectively as Anne Frank, in *The Diary of a Young Girl,* but she does point the way for every individual. Certainly each of us can respond to some challenging task, something which demands our finest creative power.

Worthy pursuits, related to creativity, become real inspiration. When we engage in them, we find meaning in life which saves us from dull drudgery.

Such inspiration can deliver us from being defeated by the crushing burden of daily chores. When a housewife shouts: "Wipe your feet! Don't tear the place apart! Leave that alone; you'll break it!" she may think she is devoted to a lovely home. Actually, she is losing the *loveliness of her home.* She is showing that her chores constitute thankless toil, which is crushing her soul, so that she has little time left for comradeship and kindliness of disposition. She is missing the joy of living by never learning the relationships of neatness and meanness, companionship and coldness. She is literally crushing the life out of *home* while she is cleaning her *house.*

People like this usually give more time to the foolish whims of hypercritical neighbors than they do to the fun of family fellowship. They study the styles of clothes more than they do the spiritual personalities of their children. Having lost the loveliness of inspired living, they never understand why their domestic comradeship collapses so quickly. Just as women with this attitude quite often lose their husbands, so terrific shocks of bitterness come to men who study the stock market diligently but never contemplate the meaning and message in a woman's eyes.

We have no difficulty seeing the tragic meaning of this in extreme cases. Here is a story from Mogasi Har, India. The wife of Dalip Singh, twenty-eight, refused to allow him into the house when he returned home drunk after selling their calf for two dollars. He had bought wine to fortify himself against a cold wave. When she opened the door the next morning, Mrs. Singh found Dalip frozen to death. Without discussing either the morals of drink or the ethics of family finances, all of us can surely agree that neither one of these individuals was an inspiration to the other!

Real inspiration can keep us far above the legalism of domestic duty. It lifts us to the magnificence of enriching comradeship. It comes with an authenticity which is the opposite of that doubt which a character in *The Marriage of Figaro* felt. Mozart makes this individual ask:

> You who do know
> All the heart's turns,
> Say, is it love now
> That in me burns?

Without mental and spiritual insight, we scarcely recognize love, because we think primarily of *our rights*, and the *duties of others*, thus facing the danger that defeated Xantippe, the wife of Socrates. She lost her brilliant husband because she never knew the happy and uplifting experience of lending him her mind and heart.

Without the inspiration of mind and heart, it is easy to repeat the tragedy of the wife of Pericles, the statesman who brought Athens to such great heights in its classical achievements. Thinking of her rights, instead of the happy privilege of fellowship, she lost her husband, one of the world's most famous statesmen. Pericles divorced her to marry Aspasia, the hetaira who had far more appeal both intellectually and socially.

Without inspiration, we cannot talk about the spiritual value of the Church. Without it, we do not even know the wealth of inspired domestic love. What we think we have is almost certain to end in hollow laughter or salty tears. For we have no altar in our home. And, after all, there are few attitudes more tragic than our thoughtless demands when we expect religion to pass a miracle and bestow upon our family a blessed religious home, while we ourselves are not willing to learn the majesty and mystery of happy human relationships. At odds with the Church and angry with God, because something has gone wrong in the home, we could at least be fair enough to acknowledge our failure to share encouragement of the highest character.

Inspiration, at its highest, based on *information* and *imagination,* reminds us of the work of the Holy Spirit. So, St. Paul writes there is nothing comparable to patient, understanding love. As he correctly says in his great prose poem, it is eternal! (I Corinthians 13)

No wonder a group of mature Scotch scholars had a ready answer to the question, What is the church? "The Church," they said, "is the community of those on earth and in heaven who through Jesus Christ are united in fellowship with God and with one another." Or, as another has said much more simply, but quite accurately, "The Church is made up of those who, because they love Jesus, love God, and love one another."

A young artist learned something of this sweeping truth one day when he complained to Blake that for him inspiration had so ceased there was apparently no life left in his work. Blake listened with marked courtesy. Then he turned to his wife and said: "It is so with us sometimes, is it not, for weeks together? What do we do then?" To which she replied, "We kneel down and pray."

IV. Dedication

If we sincerely desire to rise high enough to cultivate this kind of worship in our homes, which makes for such fortunate relationships, we will magnify the divine Other, God. He it is who transcends all programs, all schedules, and all individual desires. This means honest, wholehearted *dedication* to Christ. It is the portrayal of spirituality. The particular term we use, of course, is of secondary consideration.

"Our shared doubts have been the only thing we had in common. They are not enough." This is the conclusion a husband reached when he and his wife were engaged in a postmortem analysis following the breakup of their home. He is right. Shared doubts are never a substitute for the unifying force of faith.

Either as a member of the family, or as an individual, the most desperate battle in which we engage is one in which we keep faith in God. Our daily struggle, therefore, is between good and evil, honor and dishonor, right and wrong. Each of us will be constantly torn by inner conflict, unless we choose the side of right with all our strength. Certainly this is what we do when dedication makes our homes places worthy of worship. This is why, at our best, we want to commit ourselves to the redemptive process in our homes. We become part of the spiritual company who accept the saving spirit of Christ.

The experience and the practical demonstration of such fortunate relationships are of indispensable importance. We shall never outgrow them in a world like ours.

So, here we quickly see the pronounced value of membership in some church. Apropos of this, recall the tribute Rufus Jones paid his parents when he declared that he was "sprinkled from morning till night with the dew of religion. We never ate a meal without a family gathering, the reading of a chapter in the Bible followed by a period of silent worship when we talked with God, not far away, but very near." Thus, we also see the importance of the members of a family belonging to, and attending, the same church, whenever this is possible. Unity of home life is a difficult achievement at best; everything that promotes and cultivates happy fellowship in the home is of inestimable value.

Most important, of course, is belief in, and response to, divine Help, which is far above—and infinitely greater than—mere human aid. With this assistance of God, we can eagerly anticipate the development of Christian conscience, Christian concern, and Christian character. Love is real where there are demonstrated the gracious attitudes of which St. Paul writes in I Corinthians 13.

In such homes we create an atmosphere in which we can believe in the forgiveness of God, thus experiencing fellowship with the Highest. In this way we make it possible for the family to cultivate the continuing presence of the Divine. As we develop hospitality of mind and heart for each member of the family, we create a home in which religion can become real. More than this, wherever we go to study, work, or play, we carry with us the mood, temperament, and atmosphere of this Christian church in our house. Augustine puts it simply and brilliantly: "Not by our feet, but by our affections, we are to leave Thee or return to Thee."

This means that the experience of a united family in itself is not enough. *Our eternal unity is in God.* For the family, like the Church, is to become a redemptive fellowship. The family which is united, integrated, around and in God, by the power and presence of His Holy Spirit, can survive and help save civilization. This is because the family, as a church, is directed by a divine purpose which is eternal.

Religious idealism, then, becomes daily realism. In building a church in our homes today, we gain at least some justified hope for Christian civilization tomorrow.

A humble Finnish woman throws light on the grandeur of such dedication. During the winter of 1939–1940, the Finns were forced back so far by the Russians that orders went out to evacuate those citizens who lived in a strip of eastern Finland. The soldiers notified this old woman early one morning that they would return at dusk to burn her home. They explained that they could not permit the Russians to use any Finnish houses for shelter. When the soldiers returned, they found the poor woman's few belongings piled on a two-wheeled cart. Going into the cabin, the soldiers found the elderly woman, down on her knees, scrubbing the floor of the hut. "Mother," one of them asked, "don't you know that we have to burn the hut now? Why are you washing the floor?" Her reply was: "If it is to go for Finland, it must be the best I have to give."

If my home is to be a sanctuary for God, and a foundation for civilization, it must be the best I can make it!

SUMMARY

Happy homes are not the result of miracles.
They are attained by definite rules.

I. **We must seek *information* regarding ourselves**
    And each member of our family. This demands
    . Study of our personal, social, and sexual differences.

II. **Facts are not enough.**
    1. We must also exercise *imagination*.
    2. This practice cultivates the habit
       Of putting ourselves in the places of others.
    3. We see what they see, feel with them,
       And share their pain, sorrow, and gladness.

III. **A third requisite is *inspiration*.**
    1. This changes dullness into interest
       And accomplishment.
    2. We work together—and individually—
       In avocations.
    3. This is an unlimited field:
       Art, painting, writing, music, gardening, and so on.
    4. By means of inspiration, secular and religious
       Service become happy experiences.

IV. **The highest requisite for a happy home is:**
    Dedication to God.
    1. Thus, home becomes a place of worship
       For every member of the family.

2. Actually, such a home becomes a church

3. Where, together, all members of the family receive God's help.

VIII

We Take Christ Seriously

"The Galilean is too great for our small hearts." These words of H. G. Wells are not merely moving; they are severely painful. This is not essentially because they are true, although we should be well aware of their accuracy. Rather it is because entirely too many of us have never taken time to realize just how true they are. Instead of taking Christ seriously, we have *taken him for granted.* This is so much easier to do. Millions of us have never intended earnestly to study either the challenge of Christ or the implications of his divine demands. His words have simply not stabbed us wide-awake.

Nevertheless, because we are acquainted with Christ, we cannot possibly escape the question, Dare we take him seriously? Those who insist that they have no plans to study his life with care have already dealt with the issue. They thereby indicate that it is not their purpose to face Christ with complete honesty. All of us, however, must give attention to the words of Jesus, either sincerely or superficially.

Certainly both fairness and good sense demand that we do nothing less than *hear* him—that we at least listen attentively to what he has to say.

I. We Consider the Challenge

If we decide to do this, we know that, with complete candor, we must search for the meaning of this challenge: "If any man will come after me . . ." It is at the center of everything Jesus says—and does. We can never study Christianity with entire mental integrity until we are ready to give eager attention to these words.

Here is an arresting demand of the most exacting nature. Unfortunately, too many of us fail to ponder it because we are primarily interested in certain advantages we believe Christ offers. We do not try to understand what he is. To receive his best, means accepting *him*. Furthermore, we do not really want him, until we see in him that which we desire.

The beginning of mental honesty is, of course, an attempt to understand whatever is necessarily involved in any subject considered. In this particular instance, it has to do with Jesus and his ideas of life. Whether we agree with him or not, however, we can respect what he says. Only as we face the compelling challenge with which he dares us, do we even contemplate doing this—much less treating him as a friend. This means that we must first decide whether we desire to study Christ. Even an objective attitude begins with an honest examination of the demand and appeal he makes. The unexamined character, or cause, will never challenge us.

It is true that Jesus pointed out that we must become as children if we are to learn the worth of his causes. We must ponder his words with open minds, eagerness to learn, desire to discover—that is, with mental hospitality. This is only another illustration of how Jesus always talked plainly, as a mature person to mature people. If anyone is planning to come after me, Christ insisted, let him carefully investigate what such a decision involves.

Luther must have had something of the sweeping seriousness of this in mind when he wrote: "I will say one thing boldly and freely. Nobody in this life is nearer to God than those who hate and deny Him, and He has no more dear children than these." Whether we agree with Luther or not, the least thing we can say about such people is that they take religion seriously. For there is a passion of doubt. It necessitates earnest-mindedness.

Only as we use our minds do we learn any truth. Thus do we avoid the mistake suggested by the familiar words of Horatio in *Hamlet*. Bernardo shouts, "What, is Horatio there?" His friend replies, "A piece of him." If we are fair to Christ, we shall lend him our minds, without reservation. Only to the degree that we exercise all our intellect do we gain the right to discuss his teachings.

Many critics, to be sure, quickly complain that if our world is no better than it is at the present moment, morally and ethically, after nearly two thousand years in which we have had Christianity, the religion Jesus commended and demonstrated cannot be a very satisfactory one. Further examination is unnecessary.

But, as J. B. Phillips has quite correctly insisted, these critics make a ridiculous mistake. Christianity has never really been accepted on a large scale. It has never been in a position to control the thinking and acting of most people. It is true that its influence has been far from negligible, but it should be judged as a failure only when it has failed following its acceptance. These facts make serious study of what Christianity actually is all the more imperative.

Quite truthfully, hosts of Church members have not been willing to listen to Jesus' words with complete honesty, much less to apply these to themselves. We do not understand what is involved because we have not dared to think clearly of what he said. If, however, we consider Christ with fairness, it will be with keen minds that weigh and evaluate what he means whenever he speaks.

This is very difficult, for, as Sir Joshua Reynolds has warned, "There is scarcely any expedient to which man will not resort in order to abate and shuffle off real labor—the real labor of thinking." We may not see this fact reflected in our own attitudes. But we can understand it in others when they refuse to face truth we have long accepted! It would be preferable to display the frankness of a student who, when asked why he did not arise early to study, replied, "Because I prefer sleeping."

Years ago it was a deep desire to learn which impelled Holman Hunt to acquire facts which enabled him to paint with authority and conviction. Certain of his artist friends insisted that it was absurd for him even to consider painting Christ. "You can paint only what you see," they declared, referring to the principle of their own school of painting. "You will only waste your time trying to do the impossible," they added. "But," replied Hunt, "I am going to *see* him. I will work by his side in the carpenter's shop. I will walk with him over the hills of Galilee. I will go with him among the poor, the blind, the lame and the lepers. I will go to Gethsemane with him. I will travel with him to Calvary and climb to the cross with him, until I *see* him, and then I will paint him." Those who, with insight and appreciation, have examined some of Hunt's famous works, including "The Light of the World," are confident he accomplished his purpose.

Although we may not pay the price Holman Hunt did in studying Christ, we have no right to profess total ignorance with regard to him or his challenge. There is, to be sure, an agnosticism which can be fairly reverent. When we say we do not know Christ, we may be swayed by honest doubt. The more familiar type of agnosticism goes further and causes one to declare that he does not know, and then dogmatically to add that no one can know. . . . This individual is too sure of his knowledge! A third interpretation is to say that we do not know and that, further-more, we do not care to know.

There is, fortunately, still another possible attitude. When we confess our lack of knowledge, we can wistfully add, *"How we wish we did know!"* This was manifestly the spirit of Thomas. Always the earnest doubters have had a deep desire to learn divine truth. They have had searching minds.

This attitude is the fair one to assume. We may say that we do not know all that Christ demands of us but that we are eager to know. For this reason we listen intently to him. Indeed, we can go beyond this point, and say that although we are without that knowledge which we need, we are determined to gain it. If we sincerely mean this, it will be necessary to live with him until we understand him.

Here is truly a master of life—one who died just as he had lived, thinking of others, forgiving his enemies, and committing himself to God day after day. His whole life demands fair exami-nation—and honest appraisal.

II. Counting the Cost

This greatness of Jesus gives him the right to say: If any man will come after me, let him weigh my words. Let him examine my whole life, so he can accurately count the cost. In this way we can see Christ. We can also hear what he has to say. And every time we investigate Christ's challenge we learn far more than we anticipated. This is why Jesus insists that we carefully calculate the risk of accepting his leadership.

When some would have eagerly rushed after him, Jesus stopped and calmly asked that they frankly face the facts. He wanted them to understand what they were doing. "The foxes have holes, and the birds of the air have nests; but the Son of man hath not where to lay his head" (Matthew 8:20). Frequently using the vivid language familiar to his Eastern world, he made his point unmistakably clear. He insisted: "He that loveth father or mother more than me is not worthy of me" (Matthew 10:37).

When the full impact of his words penetrates our minds and hearts, our first impulse may be to turn away. The demand may be too great. If, however, we are able to exercise deliberate judgment, we see that loud praise is meaningless without mature understanding. "Nothing is at last sacred but the integrity of our own mind," insists Emerson, as he declares, "Whoso would be a man, must be a nonconformist." If this is essential with reference to our search for truth, it is indispensable if we are to appreciate Christ. For unless Christ matters in all areas of our lives, he does not really matter. We may not want him. But if we ever do accept him, it will be for mind, will, and heart.

Actually to live with him we must know basic facts of his character. Indeed, we have to be able to count—ethically and morally. Can we count even to two? Most of us stop at "one"— a capital "I" straight up and down. To go as far as "two," I have to say *you, another, others.*

This is the *calculated risk* of giving our hearts to goodness. For instance, I must think of the million murdered Chinese who have lost their lives because they did not accept Communism in Red China. I must think of the suffering masses of the world— hungry, cold, enslaved, persecuted—all of them, wherever they are. Berdyaev puts it this way: "The question of bread for myself is a material question, but the question of bread for my neighbor, for everybody, is a spiritual and religious question."

With Christ this concern is so comprehensive it involves every human relationship. Huxley felt the demand when he exclaimed: "It does not take much of a man to make a Christian, but it takes all there is of him."

Thackeray so clearly understood this cost that he was frequently reminded of it. One day when he and three companions were walking down the Dean Road near Edinburgh, they passed a quarry. Glancing toward a great wooden crane in the shape of a cross, Thackeray stopped and murmured one word: "Calvary." That symbol and its reality are everywhere Jesus is. If any person will come after Christ, let him count *this* cost. The least meaning it conveys involves taking upon us the sorrows, troubles, and needs of mankind!

Indeed, when we see the full import of taking Christ seriously, we discover that it is a cosmic venture. If *cosmic* sounds like a big word, it is probably because it is just that. For this two-syllable word refers to everything. Every sincere Christian *counts the cosmic cost of Christly concern.*

Surely, this cost speaks of love *for* Christ, as well as the love *of* Christ. It "is broader than the measure of man's mind," for it seeks the redemption of all mankind. No wonder a young student, who caught a glimpse of the troubles of mankind, exclaimed: "I don't see how God can stand it. I can hardly stand it myself!" Although he was discussing a paper which posed the problems of humanity, he was actually dealing with the purposes and plans of the Deity.

In his well-known play *Joan of Arc,* George Bernard Shaw catches some of the tremendous sweep and power of divine devotion when he has the Archbishop of Rheims tell Joan that she is in love with religion. As Joan's face becomes radiant, she exclaims: "I never thought of that. Is there any harm in it?" The archbishop's reply is that there is no harm but that "there is danger."

There is, indeed. Christ's love is not essentially an emotion. It is such a pronounced tendency to action that "practice is the test of its genuineness." No wonder Eric Gill declares that "a thief who loves God is a much better man than" anyone who claims to be honest but does not love. Certainly he is far more religious than any individual who insists upon truth but refuses to give God his love.

The woman of Samaria grasped something of this calculated risk. Seeing how love and its demands were vitally related to every human experience, she was tremendously excited. She ran toward her village, leaving her water pots at the well. Her eagerness to tell her friends of this strange Jew who knew so much that he was manifestly the Messiah was more intense than she understood or realized.

III. The Consequences of Commitment

Thus it becomes clear that when we take Christ seriously enough, we do not merely deliberately consider the risk involved; we also accept the consequences of committing ourselves to him. Desire for the Divine becomes ardent devotion to the Christlike character. This is an experience which we earnestly seek.

The positive principle is vital to every personal relationship. Christ makes it quite plain. "Ye are the salt of the earth: but if the salt have lost its savour, wherewith shall it be salted? . . . Ye are the light of the world. A city that is set on an hill cannot be hid. . . . Let your light so shine before men, that they may see your good works, and glorify your Father which is in heaven" (Matthew 5:13, 14, 16). "Be ye therefore perfect, even as your Father which is in heaven is perfect" (Matthew 5:48).

All superficiality is shattered when we really want to learn the meaning of such statements of Christ. They send us to some cloister to prepare our minds, hearts, and wills for the most exacting and exciting experience we can ever know.

Certainly religion, as Jesus demonstrated it, is related to every possible situation. This makes Christianity practical in every sense of the word. The twenty-fifth chapter of St. Matthew's Gospel etches this on our minds when we stop to ponder its message. Jesus here presents the acid test of religion. He makes it unmistakably plain that we shall be judged on the basis of such deeds as visiting people in prisons, clothing those who are cold because they lack adequate garments, feeding the hungry, and giving generously to those without the essentials of life. Only by incarnating the characteristics of Jesus can we ever hope to know them. Just to the degree that we act on Christ's teachings do they come to life.

As simple as this statement seems, it is difficult to accept. Apropos of this, a friend tells of a member of his church, in New York City, who upbraided his minister for visiting a man who was in one of the prisons of that city. "Some people might think a member of our church was in jail," explained the churchman. That is precisely where St. Paul was when he wrote several of his most treasured letters! "Inasmuch as ye have done it unto one of the least of these my brethren, ye have done it unto me" (Matthew 25:40) are familiar words. The idea back of them, however, is still far from "familiar" to many of us.

An eminent American statesman emphasized part of the practical issue when he spoke to a group of us in his home in Delhi. He suggested that we frankly ask ourselves what we as Americans would be willing to do to keep the friendship of India. In order to help us grasp the deeper implications of his question, he suggested that one way properly to approach this acute problem would be to consider what we would now eagerly pay to have China "on our side." We have lost China, but what would we as Americans be happy to do in order to revert to the era before the bamboo curtain came down? This suddenly brings us back to earth. The final outcome of this problem will depend upon what we actually do in Christ's spirit.

Relevant to this, following an address in his chapel, a college professor asked me, "What has Communism to offer?" Well, here is part of the answer: It depends on to whom the offer is made. It has nothing to offer me! There are, however, millions of disinherited people who obviously feel they make economic gains when they have more than they have ever possessed. Consider a news story from Peiping. It was written by Gerald Clark of the North American Newspaper Alliance. The caption of the news items was "Red China Is Amused." The paragraph referred to Chiang Kai-Shek's announcement "that he will not try to reconquer the China mainland by force."

"To many people, including . . . diplomats," wrote Mr. Clark, "it is ludicrous that Chiang ever considered such an operation. It is equally clear to any visitor that no internal 'uprising,' as reportedly anticipated by Secretary Dulles during his Formosa visit, will set the stage for a Nationalist return."

If you ask, "Why?" Mr. Clark's answer is: "The bald fact is that the present government is solidly entrenched. . . . Communism has unquestionably improved the standard of living, and this to the Asian is an essential thing. The spirit which is everywhere evident among the people is defiance against outside intrusion."

But now the sad comment is that we in the Western world could have improved the standard of living in China, had we been willing. Indeed, we would have done this—and far more—had we been Christian enough.

Apropos of this situation, James Michener says that we of the West are retreating so rapidly over Asia and Africa that we are losing 100,000,000 people to Communistic ideas every year. Should this continue, as Frank Laubach points out, within ten years there will be two billion people in Asia and Africa who hate the United States.[1] Contrast that with 500 million we may keep as our friends.

These people want to become literate. Modern farming could greatly improve their standards of living. Yet at the end of World War II we had only twenty agricultural missionaries for the whole world. In Michigan alone we had six hundred farm experts. Today we have approximately 250 agricultural missionaries for both Asia and Africa.

When we take Christ seriously we make the Fatherhood of God vivid and significant in every human experience—economic, social, and personal. We live as a family. We seek to identify ourselves with Christ. We dare not do less than this!

While visiting Bangkok, a practical implication of this came to our attention. In this city a deeply devoted missionary told

[1] In *Adult Student*, February, 1959, p. 3.

us that the one effective way we have of winning people in Thailand to Christianity is in a redemptive fellowship. Thus these wise statesmen of the church have constructed "home dormitories" in which young students can live with these devotees of the Christ, since no Christian college is permitted anywhere in Thailand. This makes it possible for these Christians to demonstrate daily the genuineness of their religion, the power of God, and the true meaning of social relationships directed by the divine Spirit of our heavenly Father. Of course, if we are to share our faith, we must have a faith to share.

Nearly two thousand years ago Jesus watched many people going through the motions of religion without accepting the might and spiritual energy of religion. In his day so few took Christ seriously. And today there are millions of churchmen who do not understand what St. Augustine meant when he said, "Thou hast touched me and I am on fire for Thy peace." Yet this is the kind of religion we dare never abandon.

Living extravagantly in our devotion to mankind means that we are baptized with Christ's spirit. When St. Paul wrote of agape, he declared that this love is eternal. It is neither mysticism nor social action, as such. It is divine passion which pursues the eternal purpose of God in every area of life.

Christ may be too great for our small hearts, but we never know true greatness until we commit ourselves to him—for this means commitment to the highest and best that life can offer. This is religion most of us have yet to demonstrate. We shall never supersede it.

The most disturbing question we now face is: Dare we *fail* to take Christ seriously? If, up to the limit of our ability, we refuse to portray the divine character of the Man who revealed God as no other person in history has been able to do, we lose eternal help of the future for all our world.

Indeed, commitment to Christ means the acceptance of both his character and his divine resources. Hear these words: "Every man who really loves me will himself be loved by my Father, and I too will love him. . . . I am not going to leave you alone in the world . . . you will realize that I am in my Father, that you are in me, and I am in you" (John 14:21, 18, 20, Phillips). Since God "never demands anything beyond His" own strength, we are ready, for we receive His power, as well as His salvation, when we dare to take Christ seriously. This is not merely timely, and now necessary; it is timeless. It is eternal.

SUMMARY

All of us have to decide whether we shall take Christ seriously.

   I. He certainly wants us to take him seriously—
      And not for granted.

  II. Fairness demands that we consider his challenge honestly.

 III. He made it so plain, we can count the cost.

      1. He spoke clearly of the requirements.

      2. The cross is at the center of Christianity.

      3. It means accepting responsibility for evils in our society.

  IV. There are consequences of commitment to Christ.

      1. They involve our treating all the world as he treated
         people.

      2. The practical test, therefore, is:

         That we have a Christlike concern for all human beings

         And for all our world.

IX

A Faith That Sings

"When they had sung an hymn, they went out into the mount of Olives." This sounds like a simple statement, relevant to an ordinary incident. Actually, it is one of the most deeply moving sentences in all literature—that is, when we understand it. Here was a small company of men going out into one of the blackest nights any group of friends had ever faced. Yet, they sang.

A heavy pall of gloom hung over them. The stars, to be sure, may have been shining with that brightness which makes the visitor to the Middle East wonder at their glory. If so, the night was all the darker, just because of that fact! In spite of this, they sang.

What hymn did they choose? How some of us would like to know! It was doubtlessly one of the Psalms with which we are familiar, for this was the hymnbook of the Jews. Was it: "I will lift up mine eyes unto the hills, from whence cometh my help. My help cometh from the Lord, which made heaven and earth"? (Psalm 121:1–2). Was it that other hymn of strong confidence: "God is our refuge and strength, a very present help in trouble"? (Psalm 46:1). It might have been a more personal testimony of ringing faith: "Yea, though I walk through the valley of the shadow of death, I will fear no evil: for thou art with me; thy rod and thy staff, they comfort me" (Psalm 23:4). It could well have been a poem of patience they sang, the kind that helps us recover our poise, when critical conditions seem to make this utterly unreasonable. "Wait on the Lord: be of good courage, and he shall strengthen thine heart: wait, I say, on the Lord" (Psalm 27:14).

In any event these men went out with a melody in their hearts. Look at them as they lift their voices in song. It seems so natural we might guess they were only concluding a lovely service of reverent worship. There they are: Facing defeat, but with no despair on their faces, and not even a suggestion of a whine in their voices. With the majesty of music on their lips, they are moving out to face the madness of a mob. With love in their hearts, they are preparing to meet men whose hatred is already hurling words of bitterness, and will later be driving nails of pain. They are demonstrating what Pliny insisted was the chief characteristic of the first century Christians. With keen insight, that Latin author writes, "They sang when they suffered."

Though they are now facing death, they have faith in life. They would have understood Joyce Kilmer, though he lived many centuries later. Not long before his own death during World War I, this brilliant young poet wrote:

> Because the road was steep and long,
>   And through a dark and lonely land,
> God set upon my lips a song,
>   And put a lantern in my hand.[1]

I. The Friends of Jesus Trusted God

What is the secret of these men? They had lived long enough with Jesus to believe there was a God capable of handling any

---

[1] From *Trees and Other Poems*, by Joyce Kilmer, copyright 1914, by Doubleday and Company. Used by permission.

possible situation, any critical conditions, no matter how difficult. Whether they had been with Christ six months or three years— the time was adequate. The scholars are not certain just how long these men had known Jesus. Whether it was months or years, they had learned enough from him to be sure of a God they could trust. This explains why these friends of Jesus lifted their voices in music, instead of collapsing at some wailing wall.

Most of us know altogether too well that we don't start out into the darkness, facing dismal defeat and death, with a song on our lips unless we have found some reason for trust.

Certainly today if we are escaping despair it is doubtlessly because we believe in a Supreme Being—One whose intelligence and power are adequate to deal with us and with our universe, or, if you want to put it more strongly, with all the worlds there are. Only with this confidence dare we lift our voices in buoyant and majestic music, night or day.

To believe in a God like this does not mean we shall be constantly hurling weighty verbal arguments against those who doubt there can be such a Deity. Those who gain this faith realize all too well that we simply do not batter our way into unbelieving minds—our own, or those of our friends. Belief is much more positive—and personal.

If our assurance is great enough to start a lyric ringing in our hearts, or keep us in tune with some majestic melody, through dreary, difficult, and dangerous days, it must include trust in a Supreme Being of worthy character and adequate power. Manifestly popular reasons for faith—statements that are shallow and superficial—are of no avail when life begins to tumble about us.

Only virile faith is essential and vital, no matter what the pragmatic test. Without this trust, there is no music for any of us.

Whatever our attitude toward this faith, even when we deny its reality, we are always expressing some kind of creed. Some insist, for instance, that dismal, unrelenting pessimism is our one possible interpretation of, and response to, the facts. Many of this number sneer at high religion. They declare it is for the mentally dumb or the moronic or, at best, the unthinking middle classes who are afraid to use their reason.

A cynical way of summarizing this was once suggested by a popular comedian when he declared that if people could glimpse the future, they would be glad to hurry back to live in the past.

Interestingly enough, the full force of our text meets us head on when we listen to words like these. C. E. Ayres once insisted that the only choice we have as reasonable people is that of becoming evangelists of despair. The phrase sounds bitter, and it obviously is. Nevertheless, it is worth pondering. For while most people do not go so far as Joseph Wood Krutch, who declares the world is finally unintelligible, we can understand how easy it is to maneuver ourselves into this predicament.

There are those who sob silently, unashamedly, wishing they could believe, but who declare they simply cannot believe in even a friendly Power in charge of the universe.

Fortunately there are those who refuse to waste precious time with sneers or sobs. Beginning a serious search for God, if there be a God, eventually they learn how to accept spiritual reality. Because God finds them at long last, they join the choir of the heroic. They unite their voices with those who sing the "Hallelujah Chorus."

These bold citizens of our world can understand the response of C. E. M. Joad when he was asked why he, who for so many years had attacked religion, denounced Christianity, and made fun of preachers, came at last humbly to request that he might be received as a member of the Anglican Church. Plainly and clearly this British philosopher replied: Our world is in too terrible a plight for man to extricate himself from this hell in which we are. It will take a God to do that!

So, while we read again the words of W. T. Stace, who says we must abandon hope in the future because there is no God in the sky to save us, we quickly recall some oft-quoted words posted on the bulletin board of a church. They concerned the health of a minister whose alert secretary used the board, which regularly carried church announcements, for the purpose of communicating the state of the minister's health. But she also continued the sentence sermons, familiar to readers. One day those who passed by the church, in autos and on the sidewalk, were startled to read:

GOD IS GOOD
DR. JONES IS BETTER

There is so much below the surface of this unwittingly facetious reference that eager minds quickly become excited with the finest reasoning of which we are capable. For there must be a God great enough to account for the greatness we can see about us. Without this confidence, we miss reason *in* life, and *for* life.

Just because trust in a divine Being of adequate wisdom and strength is relevant to this, we can understand why Voltaire said that if there were not such a Deity, we would have to invent One. For there is no peace of mind unless God gives us our minds—*and* peace.

When, however, we enter positively into the meaning of this venture, we gain insight into every description of its significance. We grasp what Sidney Lanier had in mind when he exclaimed, "God is at the organ." If He is, we can sing. Holy boldness is courage that dares to destroy despair. This is, indeed, "faith in long trousers"!

II. The Comrades of Christ Believed in Him

These men sang because they had lived with Christ long enough to believe in him. They had learned that their comrade was not merely a friend whom they admired; he was one from whom they had received more facts about life and its meaning than they had discovered anywhere, or everywhere, else. For them there was not simply a man named Jesus whom they had come to love and trust; this person had spoken to them of God as no other individual they had ever met. This knowledge had brought assurance about life which they desperately needed. No wonder they could sing!

The universe cannot produce anything greater than the universe is. Since we have Jesus Christ, we must keep remembering that at the heart of our universe there must be character as great and as good as that of Christ. There is, after all, a problem of goodness we can no more dodge than the problem of evil.

Shakespeare must be as great as *Hamlet* and *Macbeth*. One as talented as Browning is necessary to write *Saul* and *Rabbi Ben Ezra*. The one adequate explanation for Christ is a Spirit, a Cause, just as good and just as great as is he. The universe cannot produce anything finer than it is.

For this very reason some of us feel that Jesus probably made no more thrilling and dramatic statement than that almost unbelievable one which the author of the Fourth Gospel records: "He that hath seen me hath seen the Father" (John 14:9).

This is why, too, we also agree with Browning:

> That one Face, far from vanish,
>   Rather grows,
>   Or decomposes
> But to recompose.

Because Christ shows us what God is, we too can join in the majestic music of these friends of Jesus. Belief makes us bold. Faith banishes fear. Present facts help us face the future with confidence. It is now manifestly true that

> The soul can split the sky in two,
> And let the face of God shine through.[2]

So, the one question which so many thousands have wanted to ask the Sphinx—Is the universe friendly?—we raise again in the presence of Christ, and we receive our answer. In him we have both an explanation and an interpretation of the universe

[2] From *Collected Poems* by Edna St. Vincent Millay (New York, Harper & Bros.); copyright 1917–1945 by Edna St. Vincent Millay. By permission of Norma Millay Ellis.

which delivers us from despair, and thus does not simply put a lantern in our hands, but a song on our lips.

Pondering this, we speak with hushed reverence as we declare that *God was always "Christian"* but that Christ discloses this eternal fact with reason, force, and persuasion. Calvary gives us a picture of the deep regard the Deity has for humanity. Golgotha speaks of the divine care God has for people everywhere. As we gaze steadfastly on a Person strong and gracious enough to go to the cross for us, we realize that Calvary is reality and that it is also a symbol of a truth so sweeping no one of us can ever adequately describe it. Serious-minded writers, as well as popular poets, have discovered this. One both wise and widely read, Edwin Markham, suggests something of this same fact when he assures us that "love is all the law we need" and that Christ is the one God we have to know.

We have the graciousness of this dramatized in the traditional story of Christ, standing outside the gates of Heaven, shading his eyes with his hands, as he eagerly searches the horizon. He is obviously anticipating the coming of someone. The apocryphal story—which may not be as apocryphal as some have intimated—includes references to the questioning of Jesus' disciples. They ask why he does not come inside the halls of happiness and join the others in the joys of Paradise. "Why are you out there?" they ask. "I am waiting for Judas," is the reply of Jesus.

This says it forcefully enough. Indeed, it is because of Christ that we can make the words of Browning our own:

God, thou art love! I build my life on that.

This is why the friends of Jesus could sing that night, nearly two thousand years ago, when they went out into the mount of Olives.

III. Christ Believed in His Friends

Whether their hymn was like an anthem or a holy chant, it was majestic, because they had lived with Jesus long enough to see that Christ believed in *them*. Consider what a most unlikely band of men this was. Who would have then thought they would be remembered as saints or heroes? It is neither rash nor unfair to say that the men in this "motley" group were ambitious, cowardly, and jealous. James and John wanted to be accorded high seats of honor in the Kingdom. The three of the inner circle went to sleep when Jesus needed them most. Peter denied he knew his Master. And all the disciples fled that tragic night he longed for the warmth of friendship and the strength of virile love.

Yet, Christ believed in them! He told vacillating Simon Peter that it was upon his faith he would build his Church. He so transformed John, one of those who in bitterness wanted to call fire down on an inhospitable village, that he is known as the disciple of love. This is the kind of thing he was daily doing for those who walked with him, listened to his words, and believed his affirmations about God.

For Christ did not merely reveal God to us; at the same moment he shows us man at his highest and best. He himself was man. Thus he kept telling these comrades of the way what God meant for them to be, and how they could become just that. "In all history he rightly estimated the true greatness of man," declared Emerson. Actually, says Adolf von Harnack, "Jesus for the first time brought to light the supreme worth of every human being." This we see more clearly as we study history.

These facts become even more pertinent when we recall that many critics of Christianity have denounced this religion for insisting that we should confess our sins, acknowledge our weakness, and seek help outside of, above, and beyond us.

This, however, is precisely the direction to follow. For we have the possibility of accepting and receiving the divine Spirit. Power is available for us. Furthermore, as C. S. Lewis has reminded us, we do share in the victory only when we are "in the victor." [3]

[3] *The Weight of Glory* (New York, The Macmillan Company, 1949), p. 42.

An experience of Leslie Church, when he was preaching one Sunday at St. Martin's, Birmingham, England, makes this quite vivid. After the service, an elderly gentleman, exceedingly frail, stopped the minister to speak to him. "You mentioned Lord Nelson," tremblingly commented the old gentleman, to whom life had evidently not been kind. "Yes, I did," replied Dr. Church, a bit mystified by this statement of his auditor. "My grandfather held him in his arms as he died on the *Victory*," exclaimed the old man, his physical frame quivering with excitement and pride.

No longer was the frail old man a nobody in society. He was a part of all English history. He was related to the heroic and the great of Britain's long story.

In a much more realistic and vital way we become a part of all Christian history in Christ. Speaking reverently, we can say that when he holds us, by our hands or by our love, we *do* become somebody. When we hold Christ in our hearts, we are no longer insignificant and of little value, to ourselves and our world.

The friends of Jesus remind us of their having been in touch with Greatness—and Goodness, because they had been with him. More than this, even when he was betrayed and deserted Christ loved these friends and believed in them. They had felt the tug of his care and divine concern. When they failed him, therefore, most of them did not completely collapse.

This is why, though we may not fully grasp all that Sir Thomas Browne means, we can at least partly understand what he has in mind when he says: "There is surely a piece of divinity in us, something that was before the elements, and owes no homage to the sun." It is Christ who makes us aware of this.

With Christ we can face the worst and demonstrate the best. It was on the desperate struggle to cover the eighteen hundred miles between the South Pole and their base that gallant Captain Lawrence Oates, accompanying Captain Scott, became disabled. He refused to continue as a burden on his comrades. Bidding them goodbye, he deliberately walked away into a raging blizzard. He died as he had lived—heroically. There was no ecstatic vision, no public to cheer him on, and no bands were blasting martial music. But it is an act that starts all the bands playing. Oates made us see that "Courage is fear that has said its prayers."

This same heroic potential is what Robert Wicks, former Dean of Chapel, Princeton University, emphasized when he wrote of a worker who was handling a windlass, pulling up a large bucket of rocks from a deep hole where two of his comrades were working. The load reached the top, on one of its trips, when suddenly something went wrong with the controls of the machine. "The windlass reversed, dropping the bucket at a furious rate toward the heads of the men below." In a flash the man at the top realized there was no room for his fellow workers to get out of the way. "He thrust his own arm into the cog wheels clear to the shoulder—and stopped the bucket." Is it too much to say that he lost his arm but saved his soul? Maybe it is not too poetic to suggest that he disclosed a facet of divinity.

At any rate, the friends of Jesus were engaged in acts of courage and selfless daring after Calvary. They had been with Christ long enough to see that he did believe in them and that they could increasingly become divinely daring and great with a Godlike grandeur. They disclosed why Christianity does not preach the survival of the fit, but the *revival* of the *unfit*.

Our response to Calvary indicates our evaluation of God's judgment on us. But we can respond only because on the cross God in Christ is saying that man is worth dying for. He is now, or he can become, that kind of character. Having learned this about themselves, these friends of Jesus had not merely a theme for their music, but a tune that kept them in harmony with Christ.

IV. The Friends of Christ
Faced the Future Exultantly

It was this experience that brought them eternity in time. They had accepted a love that is timeless. "To be loved adds something to any man or woman," writes Robert Raynolds in *The Quality of Quiros*. Then he observes: "and so something humane had been added to Isabel; but her degree of acceptance of love was small, and she could not give without help, but needed the demand of Quiros to move her." [4]

Lift this so high it may make us dizzy to look down. From the highest altitude we dare ascend, look! For God's love is broader than the measure of our minds. His is a kindness which ours only dimly suggests. Dare we believe this? If so, we can "be still," and learn quietude, for God, who is on our side, will lead us into a joyful and blessed future.

There *is* a tomorrow, and it belongs to God. So there is God, who will be with us tomorrow. Even if man does make a fool of himself and destroy his world, God will not be destroyed. He will still be in charge of the universe. Like the first century friends of Christ, those who trust Him can sing.

[4] Pp. 303–304.

SUMMARY

The night is dark; we need *light*.

Danger is everywhere; we need *daring*.

Life becomes most depressing; we need *encouragement*.

The friends of Jesus found all these.

I. In a day as difficult for them,
As ours is for us,
They found *faith in a Divine Power*.
They lived with Jesus until they were sure
His trust in God could become theirs.

II. They knew Christ so well,
And believed him so completely,
They were certain *God was as good as Jesus*.
The universe cannot produce anything
Better than it is!

III. They were sure they could become
Better and more Godlike.
Experiencing Christ's influence,
They became confident there was a
Power great enough to make them
What they ought to be.

IV. All this meant that they were
Brave for today and tomorrow.
They could sing in the night.
So we, too, can be *dauntlessly daring*
As we face *our* future.

X

God Can Really Meet Our Needs!

"My God will supply all that you need from his glorious resources in Christ Jesus" (Philippians 4:19, Phillips).

This sentence is one of the most exciting in the New Testament. In fact, you will search a long time before you find anything comparable to it anywhere. No wonder St. Paul fairly shouts it in our ears. Our problem is not in recognizing its message, or in feeling its sweeping force. It is not even in appreciating its magnificence. Rather it is in believing in the dependability of its truth; it is, indeed, in accepting this affirmation at full face value.

Before we consider its possible accuracy, however, we do well to remind ourselves that this is not just an affirmation of a brilliant writer who knew how to make words speak clearly, shout forcefully, and sing rhythmically. This sentence is not a *text;* it is a *testimony.* Do not, therefore, center your attention on the writer of this chapter, or essentially on the words you will read, which I write. Listen to Paul! He is no research student engaged in objective analysis. He is not a scholar living in an ivory tower, far from the realities of life. He is a man of the world, who has known

trials, disappointment, disillusionment, defeat. Hear him as he
summarizes some of these experiences:

Of the Jews five times received I forty stripes save one. Thrice was I
beaten with rods, once was I stoned, thrice I suffered shipwreck, a
night and a day I have been in the deep; In journeyings often, in perils
of waters, in perils of robbers, in perils by mine own countrymen, in
perils by the heathen, in perils in the city, in perils in the wilderness,
in perils in the sea, in perils among false brethren; in weariness and
painfulness, in watchings often, in hunger and thirst, in fastings often,
in cold and nakedness. Besides those things that are without, that
which cometh upon me daily, the care of all the churches [II Corinthians 11:24–28].

I. All of Us Have Needs

Whether we believe this affirmation of Paul: that there is a
God capable of meeting us where we are, and of responding to
the deepest needs of our lives, eventually we are forced to recognize our needs. Frequently they are so pronounced that we cannot know of their severely searching character until we are swept
off our feet by some crisis. Whether, however, we see them early
or understand them late, they are real, and eventually we must
try to handle them.

We may doubt that there is any person, or any power, which
can adequately supply our deepest needs of mind and heart.
We can never escape them. We cannot deny that there are situa-
tions and conditions which severely try us, sometimes to the limit
of our strength and patience. We may honestly say that we see
no one capable of dealing with the crises of our lives, but eventually we cannot blindfold ourselves to the demand for aid which
we are unable to furnish ourselves. There are crucial moments,
critical experiences and crises that we are entirely incapable of
handling with our own resources. Furthermore, they sweep upon
us when we least expect them.

> Just when we are safest, there's a sunset-touch,
> A fancy from a flower-bell, some one's death,

A chorus-ending from Euripides,
And that's enough. . . .[1]

Sooner or later, no matter how comfortable life has been, there are hours that usher us into experiences no one with mere human strength is capable of handling. Any proof of this we need comes in living long enough to see life in its sweeping entirety.

Here is a newspaper story which suggests one emphasis of this truth: "The stout heart which beat inside Jim Thorpe as he stormed to the pinnacle of the sport's world, gave out Saturday. The Sak and Fox Indian was the greatest athlete in the last fifty years." This is the summary of an Associated Press announcement of March 29, 1953. So! No matter how strong and powerful we may be athletically, there is a day when our prowess fails us.

II. The Advantage of Awareness of Need

Only as we face our needs are we in a position to do something about them. Awareness of any physical, mental, or spiritual lack is essential to an understanding of it. It is a determining factor as to whether we are able to meet it.

Consider this man, to whom his physician says: "You have a bad heart. You must quit work." This industrial leader wisely took the advice of his expert physician. As a result, he began to follow the professional advice of a heart specialist. He learned to care for himself. He called upon medical aid whenever it was necessary. By disciplining himself, he is living much longer than many of his friends who were not aware that anything was physically wrong with them. Because he faced his needs and did something about them, he is gaining years of blessedness he would not have known otherwise.

Physicians have been telling us that many people would be better off with some organic trouble, provided they were aware of it, and learned how to handle it with discretion and an applica-

[1] Robert Browning, "Bishop Blougram's Apology."

tion of the resources at hand. Unfortunately, hosts of people refuse to recognize their needs. Consequently, their condition is much more serious than they think.

Dentists deal with the same principle when they tell us that we should brush our teeth three times a day and see our dentist twice a year. This is their way of saying that we must face certain facts if we are to keep good teeth. We must recognize the need for caring for them.

In each of these instances we have a suggestion of far more important needs which concern minds, attitudes, will, and character itself. No one of us can escape them. It is advantageous to face them and at least try to do something about them.

III. The Reality of Divine Resources

Whatever our deepest needs are, the *response of help* can be just as real as the *demand for help*. The divine Aid upon which we can call, says Paul, is more than adequate for crises, for those severely exacting demands which, at some time, we are forced to face.

There are, to be sure, many who feel that both Paul and others who apparently express the same confidence he emphasizes are not dealing realistically with life. Our attitude, however, toward this truth, or indeed our attitude toward any truth, *does not change facts*. It determines only whether we receive the benefits of them. He who laughs last always laughs best, and those who know what to do with regard to life's problems, and who follow the direction in which their spiritual insight points, achieve wisdom which brings the deepest satisfaction.

Consider the story of numerous efforts to conquer yellow fever. Recall what the scientists and doctors finally learned—basic facts which those concerned with diseases now happily accept. We learned that the germ of yellow fever is carried by a *mosquito*, by a *female* of a *particular species* of mosquito. She must receive the germ from some sufferer of yellow fever *at a particular period in the time of his suffering*. She must carry the infection in her body for *a specified length of time*. Then, and then only, can the female successfully inject the poisonous germ into the body of a formerly healthy person.

It is easy to smile condescendingly about these facts. Many people have indulged in this strange sense of humor. Indeed, when the first announcements of how to handle this death-dealing disease were made, some laughed hilariously at these "facetious" statements with regard to yellow fever. If these discoveries had been broadcast in our day, probably some well-known comedians on television would have lasted longer, since their script writers could have used this additional theme as a basis of humor. Some of them might have had a rollicking time, using the wisecrack to point out that "the female is more deadly than the male."

Laughing at scientific facts, however, was not—and never is —the effective technique for dealing with a dread disease. When we decided to get rid of yellow fever, we were forced to go in the direction in which the keenest-minded scientists and physicians advised us to proceed. After our indulgence in fun, when we finally quit laughing—because we wanted to be rid of yellow fever —we were compelled to accept the facts to which I have referred —and then use them.

Proceeding to act on truth is always of supreme importance. It is not enough to know that there is help for us. We must receive, eagerly accept, and use, that aid which is available. "He that doeth the will shall know the doctrine." A number of years ago, a speaker in Hyde Park, London, emphasized this forcefully one day when he was insisting upon the power and grace of Christianity. A heckler in the audience shouted: "We've had Christianity two thousand years, and look at the state of the world!" "Yes," the speaker retorted, "and we have also had water a million years, and look at your dirty face!" We must apply a principle or purpose, and actually use a power, for it to become effective. Eventually its worth can be seen in our practical demonstration of its character.

IV. Equipped for the Unexpected

Thus our greatest need is equipment for the unexpected. If we knew exactly what was going to occur, we might be able to handle many conditions with greater skill, more finesse, and happier confidence. But we never know what is immediately ahead of us. Life is a conglomeration of so many occurrences, so many accidents! It is made up of day and night, joy and sorrow, peace and pain. We are prepared for today or tomorrow only as we are equipped for that about which we may not have thought, of which we may never have even dreamed, and concerning which we may have had only one ardent desire; namely, to avoid the specific difficulty.

Dean Wicks of Princeton Chapel often stressed this in a story he told of certain fox hunters who were members of a club in New Jersey. When these individuals agreed upon the time for hunting, they directed those in charge of their horses to bring them out, saddled and ready. The men and women were clad in attire of variegated colors, with red and green predominant. There were registered hounds of such superb training that the hunters had complete confidence in them. At the last moment before the hunt, a servant in the club dragged the skin of a dead fox across the fields over which they planned to ride.

One day, quite unexpectedly, a live fox crossed the trail. The fine blooded hounds were off with new excitement, barking with "musical rhythm" that thrilled the riders. The horses galloped after the hounds. Riders who had never had any idea of galloping off to where they went that day suddenly faced conditions altogether different from what they had anticipated. The ditches were broader than any they had ever tried to jump. There were higher fences to be scaled, and hedges to be cleared, out of all proportion to those the hunters had previously been compelled to negotiate. Women were left sprawled on the green grass, unable to manage the ditches that had to be jumped. Men were rudely knocked from their saddles by the limbs of trees in the woods through which the horses raced as they followed the barking hounds.

Life is like that! The unexpected, the unplanned, and the unanticipated are before us, whoever we are. We are not ready for today or tomorrow until we are equipped for it. We cannot know what we shall have to encounter.

In a popular drama a playwright had one of his characters say that the only certainty in life is uncertainty. It is obvious that this author had hit upon something very significant and penetrating. With regard to his succinct statement, my comment is: *The only certainty with which to meet life's uncertainties is God.* It is of the importance of this fact that Paul was thinking when he said: "My God will supply all that you need from His glorious resources in Christ Jesus."

V. *Power for Every Need*

The startling assurance in this affirmation is the insistence of Paul that there is power by means of which we can meet *every* possible need. If we could only accept this, how different life would be! Happily, hosts of people have come to discover that there *are* dependable resources and that they are available.

A scholarly Scotchman, who had been defeated by drink, caught a glimpse of how this can affect our whole life. The incident occurred one day as Henry Drummond was leaving the home of some friends in the hills of Scotland. The host of Mr. Drummond told him that he and his wife were not going to accompany their guest to the village, where he would catch the train for his next appointment. "Our coachman is a very wonderful man and quite an unusual scholar, but he has been defeated by drink," they told Mr. Drummond, "and we hope you may have an opportunity to say something to him that will help him."

Henry Drummond climbed up onto the seat next to the coachman, and before the driver realized what was happening, Mr. Drummond had won his way into the coachman's mind and heart. The driver was confessing his failures and expressing regret for the collapse which had so tragically torn his life. "Suppose," said Mr. Drummond, "as we ride along these curves and hills, the horses you are driving got out of control. Then you suddenly realized you could not manage them. In a flash, however, you recalled that the man who sat beside you was the finest horseman in Scotland and that there had never been a span of horses which he could not control. What would you do?" "Oh," exclaimed the coachman, "is that what Christ expects me to do?" "Exactly!" replied Henry Drummond. "Turn the reins of your life over to him!"

This is precisely what Paul did. He turned over his entire life to God in Christ, to the Christlike God. It was this experience which made him sure that there is no condition which the power of God is not capable of meeting and handling.

I repeat: All of us have needs. They may be quite different from those of the coachman. We may not even acknowledge some of them to our intimate friends. But there they are! We do have to deal with them.

It may be a bad disposition. It may be an unmastered temper. It may be a tongue that we cannot control, about which James wrote so vividly when he said: "The human tongue is physically small, but what tremendous effects it can boast of! A whole forest can be set ablaze by a tiny spark of fire, and the tongue is as dangerous as any fire, with vast potentialities for evil. It can poison the whole body; it can make the whole of life a blazing hell" (James 3:5, 6).[2]

[2] J. B. Phillips, *The New Testament in Modern English* (New York, The Macmillan Company, 1958).

> In the heat of passion I uttered words
>   That wounded the heart of a friend.
> I would have given worlds to have called them back,
>   But to sue for pardon I could not bend.
>
> So I battled on, till the pain in my heart
>   Grew so great I wildly fled,
> To find my friend and pardon crave;
>   I was too late; my friend was dead.

Not dead physically, but dead as far as I was concerned. I would never have entrée to his mind, his heart, his love.

It may be that some moral failure has disturbed us. Recall what happens, how weak we become, when we collapse ethically, feeling utterly helpless in the face of overwhelming odds. Eventually, we are compelled to confess our human weakness.

I am thinking of this as I remember a knock that sounded at my study door one night. A young man was seeking help. A few sentences revealed how intricately involved his difficulty was. It was clear that he needed a specialist. A Christian psychiatrist was manifestly his hope, but one was not available at the moment. So discouraged was he that he earnestly sought my aid even though I was not properly trained to handle his very complicated problem. In his desperation he began to glimpse the necessity of turning to Help higher than that which is human, strength which is mightier than any we know as individuals.

Some days later, he walked down the aisle of the sanctuary to unite with the Church. As I watched him kneel at the altar during a Maundy Thursday Communion Service, I confess I was deeply moved. His God was meeting his need.

Each of us eventually faces conditions that demand resources greater than his own. Many of us, to be sure, at the moment may be very proud of how modern we are. We may insist we do not suffer from any deep sense of *guilt* and *shame*, such as our forefathers described. But, as has been so forcefully and frequently pointed out, we are nevertheless often troubled by a *sense of frustration* and a *lack of resources for life.*

Whatever our need, exclaims Paul, God is able to meet it! This is the testimony of a man who would have been as completely discouraged and defeated as many of us are, had he not discovered a might greater than his own. God can meet any situation, he insists, no matter how difficult, no matter how intricately involved, or how fraught with danger.

Here is a woman who also discovered this exciting truth. She attended the church of R. J. Campbell before that minister moved to London. In an unexpected way, she discovered the same source of power Paul knew. Because she earned her living by singing, she felt it was necessary to face the footlights one evening when her child was critically ill. As the notes of her last song sank into silence, the crowd burst into applause so vigorously that their demand for an encore went far beyond mere politeness. The mind of the young singer, however, was upon her child. Eager to get away from the footlights, she rushed home.

When she arrived, her physician was waiting. He kindly explained that her child was critically ill but that the girl would recognize her. She could go in and talk quietly with her, but with the understanding that the time was short. The first request of the child was, "Mummie, sing to me." The mother who had fled from the footlights because she could not bear to sing an encore stooped over the bed, lifted the child, and walked the floor singing:

> I think when I read that sweet story of old,
>   When Jesus was here among men,
> How He called little children as lambs to His fold,
>   I should have liked to have been with them then.

You say: "Wait! Now you are talking about death. All through this chapter we have been interested because you have been dealing with life—practical everyday matters. *This* is the kind of religion that concerns us!" My answer is: I am still talking about life, the inescapable experiences of our daily existence. Do not be alarmed about the little girl. If we accept the teachings of Christ, we agree that God loves and receives little children. It was "Mummie" who had to go on living, who needed the resources of God, the sustaining power of love, the assurance of divine Grace. The mother was in need of equipment for life, preparation for something she had not anticipated . . . and so shall we all!

Indeed, we can now know at least something of many inevitable experiences for which we must prepare. To some degree we can be aware of what is ahead for us. Old age is one of them. The only way to avoid this is to die young. But God is capable of helping us then.

> E'en down to old age all My people shall prove
> My sovereign, eternal, unchangeable love;
> And when hoary hairs shall their temples adorn,
> Like lambs they shall still in My bosom be borne.

> When through the deep waters I call thee to go,
> The rivers of woe shall not thee overflow;
> For I will be with thee thy troubles to bless,
> And sanctify to thee thy deepest distress.[3]

Dwight L. Moody suggested the practical reality of this experience. Because he knew so much about the grace of God that few of us have ever been able to demonstrate confidence as vividly as did he, one day a friend asked him if he had "dying grace." "Oh, no!" exclaimed Mr. Moody. "I have living grace, and when the time comes that I will need it, I am sure that God will also give me dying grace."

This is the attitude and spirit of those who accept the resources of God, about which St. Paul spoke so plainly because he knew them so well. Whatever happens, whenever it occurs, we

---

[3] From the hymn "How Firm a Foundation."

know there is a Person who cares, whose power is adequate to meet every situation we may face. This is the thrilling and exciting truth of Christianity. This is St. Paul's testimony. There are tens of thousands of people who have demonstrated its dependability. Often this is so vivid and dramatic that we do not merely find it out of order to deny its reality; we happily accept it, and eagerly try to learn its deeper meaning.

Sooner or later, we do have to experience death. During the closing hours of O. Henry's life, when he was in a semiconscious state, he called out: "Nurse! Nurse!" As the young woman came hurrying into his room, to the side of his bed, she asked what her patient wanted. O. Henry replied: "Bring me a candle." "Why do you want a candle, sir?" "I'm afraid to go home in the dark."

No matter when, or under what circumstances, we face the dangerous and difficult hours of life, at the close of our physical existence we do not have to go home in the dark! With the grace, power, and light of divine Love, even though we may not know technical music, or the skill of talented singers, we can join all these, as we go home singing:

> Sun of my soul, Thou Saviour dear,
> It is not night if Thou be near:
> O may no earthborn cloud arise
> To hide Thee from Thy servant's eyes.

"My God will supply all that you need from His glorious resources in Christ Jesus."

SUMMARY

I. All of us have needs.
The fact that we are at times unaware of them
Makes them even more pronounced.

II. Our awareness of needs may direct us to seek help.
Of course, any available aid is advantageous
To the degree we accept it.

III. Divine help is as real as human need,
But no one can claim this for another.

IV. Life is filled with the unexpected.
Divine power is adequate for the uncertainties we face.
For the great certainty of life is GOD.
He has power for us.

V. Whatever my need, God can meet it.
If defeated by drink, an uncontrolled tongue,
Temper, moral collapse, sorrow, old age,
Even by fear of death—
God has POWER for us.
With Him we can conquer
And live *victoriously*.

Prayer

Help me, O God, to accept the gift of Thy divine grace. Where I am confused in my thoughts, give me clarity of judgment; where I am weak, make me strong; where I have depended upon human resources, give me such a desire for Thy divine power that my own life will be a testimony to Strength that can cope with any condition. Above all, give me the character, the love, and spirit of Jesus Christ. For all these I offer my gratitude, which grows greater with every experience of Thy divine goodness. Amen.

Date Due

BROADMAN
B P
SUPPLIES

Code 4386-04, CLS-4, Broadman Supplies, Nashville, Tenn.,
Printed in U.S.A.